Routledge Revivals

World Disorder and Reconstruction

First published in 1932, *World Disorder and Reconstruction* provides an examination of the global economic crisis of the era. The book delves into the causes of the Great Depression, analyzes the international situation as it stood, and outlines the necessary measures for recovery alongside the forces already working toward economic restoration. Written in straightforward language without compromising scientific rigor, it offers readers a clear understanding of the challenges and solutions of the time. In its concluding chapter, the author shares insights into what he believed to be the ultimate trajectory and implications of contemporary developments. This work serves as an invaluable resource for students and researchers specialising in economic history.

World Disorder and Reconstruction
An Epitome of the Economic Situation

Hubert Blake

First published in 1932
by George Allen & Unwin Ltd

This edition first published in 2025 by Routledge
4 Park Square, Milton Park, Abingdon, Oxon, OX14 4RN

and by Routledge
605 Third Avenue, New York, NY 10158

Routledge is an imprint of the Taylor & Francis Group, an informa business

© 1932 Hubert Blake

All rights reserved. No part of this book may be reprinted or reproduced or utilised in any form or by any electronic, mechanical, or other means, now known or hereafter invented, including photocopying and recording, or in any information storage or retrieval system, without permission in writing from the publishers.

Publisher's Note
The publisher has gone to great lengths to ensure the quality of this reprint but points out that some imperfections in the original copies may be apparent.

Disclaimer
The publisher has made every effort to trace copyright holders and welcomes correspondence from those they have been unable to contact.

A Library of Congress record exists under LCCN: 33006188

ISBN: 978-1-041-14529-5 (hbk)
ISBN: 978-1-003-67500-6 (ebk)
ISBN: 978-1-041-14571-4 (pbk)

Book DOI 10.4324/9781003675006

WORLD DISORDER AND RECONSTRUCTION

AN EPITOME OF THE ECONOMIC SITUATION

by

HUBERT BLAKE

LONDON
GEORGE ALLEN & UNWIN LTD
MUSEUM STREET

FIRST PUBLISHED IN 1932

All rights reserved
PRINTED IN GREAT BRITAIN BY
UNWIN BROTHERS LTD., WOKING

PREFACE

People everywhere, and business men in particular, are endeavouring to frame their views on the current position and outlook. The complexity of the issues involved, however, is such that the prime difficulty is to see the situation as a whole.

The attempt has here been made in the shortest possible compass to trace the causes of the crisis, to outline the existing situation and to consider the conditions and prospects of revival.

In the last chapter—which is, no doubt, controversial—some further reflections have been offered on what are conceived to be the outlines of future economic evolution.

I particularly wish to thank Mr. P. B. Whale, B.Sc. (Econ.), M.Com., and Mr. Clifford T. Smith, B.Sc. (Econ.), for their valued counsel on particular problems, but, in so doing, I do not wish to involve them in any responsibility for opinions that I have expressed. My warm thanks are also due to those who have kindly helped me by reading the proofs.

HUBERT BLAKE

PALMERSTON HOUSE
    LONDON, E.C.
       June 1932

CONTENTS

CHAPTER	PAGE
PREFACE	5
I. THE FUNDAMENTAL CAUSES OF THE WORLD SLUMP	9
II. MONETARY CHAOS AND THE FALL IN THE PRICE LEVEL	56
III. A BLESSING IN DISGUISE	79
IV. REPERCUSSIONS ABROAD, AND THE EXTERNAL SITUATION GENERALLY	102
V. OUTLINES OF A CONSTRUCTIVE SOLUTION	128
VI. A WORLD IN TRANSITION	151
STATISTICAL APPENDIX	177
INDEX	185

WORLD DISORDER AND RECONSTRUCTION

CHAPTER I

THE FUNDAMENTAL CAUSES OF THE WORLD SLUMP

Of late years analysis and explanation in most fields of enquiry have to commence with the effects of the War. The Great War was not only a gigantic military operation involving suffering and death on a scale hitherto unknown, but one of the profoundest economic disturbances in history, the effects of which were only fully revealed after hostilities had ceased. When considering the causes of the present great depression which began at the end of 1929, it is well to remember that the world has never fully regained its balance after the War-time upheaval.

The fact is, nevertheless, plain that the disorders in the economic system, however severe, did not prevent substantial headway being made in the period 1925-28. Indeed, the progress was far beyond what could have reasonably been foretold by an observer taking stock of the situation about the year 1921—that is after the post-War boom had collapsed. It is, therefore, advisable to regard the undoubted persistence of War-time dislocation as a pre-disposing condition to the present slump rather than as a cause. The economic structure was ill-compacted when called upon to bear unprecedented stresses. It was like a ship caught in a storm at sea with the cargo badly stowed. The ship would not founder by reason of the storm alone, nor would the cargo break loose without the storm. But when the two are in conjunction destruction is threatened.

It will be well to cast a brief glance at the legacy of disorder left from the War.

The most obvious is the special direction given to industry by War-time requirements. Particular industries were expanded to secure a volume of production that has never since been required of them. Collieries, blast furnaces and shipyards that were working to capacity during the War have not again been in full employment, if they have been employed at all. The late Sir Hugh Bell pointed out that the plant extensions to steelworks demanded by the Government programme in the latter period of the War were only completed after the War ended, and thus increased capacity at a time when demand was about to undergo substantial reduction.

What applies to the metal, engineering and shipbuilding industries in particular, applies to all others in part. It was inevitable that a lack of correspondence with the needs of peace-time requirements should be revealed after several years' prosecution of a particular and different aim to the exclusion of all other considerations. When traders and manufacturers sought to pursue their business after the manner of pre-War practice, they found that many things had happened in the interval. For one thing, new processes had been introduced. The coal industry, for example, soon found that it had to contend not only with the competition of oil and electricity, but with fuel economy inventions and new sources of supply. Nor was it possible to resume the old trading relationships as they were when interrupted. In the interval others had stepped into the breach and were not easily dislodged, as Lancashire knows to her cost. More important still, the closing of some of the great manufacturing centres to the outer world had given an immense stimulus to the development of home manufactures in countries previously dependent on external supply. Manufacturing expansion thus occurred in two different directions; in that of the great manufacturing nations straining to fulfil military requirements; in that of other countries learning to supply their own needs. It has been estimated that manufacturing capacity during the War about doubled.

The industrial disorganization, though severe, was less harmful than the financial chaos that paradoxically followed close upon the return of peace. The financial problem was left alone during the War to be decided afterwards as best it might be. During the War the Exchanges were pegged, sterling on the dollar, francs and lire on sterling, and so on. The cost of providing English and Continental buyers with the dollars and sterling required to maintain the Exchanges at the pegged level constitutes the War debts that have ever since clogged the exchange system, and which are included below as one of the main causes of the financial breakdown. But apart from this particular aspect the handed-down cost of the War must, in any case, have burdened the whole economic system. Internal debts, high taxation, the adjustment of the foreign exchanges to post-War levels, all these were economic penalties which had to be paid and are still being paid.

An important and special aspect of the financial muddle left over from the War is the deplorable fall in silver, the currency of a large part of Asia and of Mexico. After the War silver reached so high a price that the silver content of the coinage in gold-standard countries was worth more in the market than its nominal value. Coins were melted down in order to extract a profit by the sale of the pure metal. Several European countries were thus compelled to reduce the silver content of their subsidiary coinage, which left them with considerable surplus stocks of metal which from time to time have been realized. A somewhat similar position arose in India. During the War the Indian Government was compelled to make very large purchases of silver, owing to the reluctance of the population to accept paper money. After the War this attitude changed and paper

THE FUNDAMENTAL CAUSES OF THE WORLD SLUMP

money again circulated. The Government's silver requirements were, therefore, diminished by this factor, and subsequently by the adoption of the gold-bullion standard in 1920, and by the value of the rupee being fixed at 1s. 6d. instead of 1s. 4d. The Indian Government in this way became possessed of an unwanted accumulation of silver and has, therefore, been a consistent and large seller over a period of years as opportunity has offered. The Siamese Government having substituted a gold-standard currency for that of silver, has also been a seller. The result of all this has been a tremendous fall in the price of the metal. From the high level reached in 1920 of $89\frac{1}{2}$d. per oz., the price steadily declined until a low level of 12d. per oz. was touched in early 1931. The effect on Eastern trade was very similar to that of a rapidly depreciating paper currency. Purchasing power was diminished and exports received a febrile stimulus, with resultant dislocation to world trade.

The various disturbances enumerated would in themselves provide a partial explanation of the existence of another special post-War problem, namely, the substantially higher ratio of unemployed persons which has marked even the relatively prosperous years since the War, and which, while chiefly a most distressing human problem, has additionally, of course, important economic bearings in wasted productive capacity and financial cost.

Adequate evidence has been offered to support the statement that the world has never fully recovered from the effects of the War. But that the continuing disorganization was not decisive is proved by the rapid progress of 1925–28. It did, however, tend to weaken the power of the economic organism to withstand the buffeting it subsequently received. The after-effects of the War are thus best regarded as pre-disposing conditions.

The question is "What were the injurious factors which not only checked further progress, but plunged the world into a profound depression from which it has so far been unable to recover?"

From the entanglement of intermingling influences it seems possible to distinguish the following as predominant, each of which demands special attention:

Relative Over-Production of an important group of Primary Commodities.
Failure to observe the conditions necessary for the successful functioning of the international Gold Standard.
The special influence of War debts and Reparations.
The Wall Street Crash.

RELATIVE OVER-PRODUCTION OF CERTAIN COMMODITIES

Everybody recognizes that there can be no such thing as general over-production while the wants of mankind remain unsatisfied. The greater part of the world's population, despite a heightened standard of living, touch

THE FUNDAMENTAL CAUSES OF THE WORLD SLUMP

only the fringes of economic satisfaction. The four great industrial countries between them have an army of over twenty-five million unemployed to whom the same comment applies. What can and does happen is that the component parts of the industrial whole fail to maintain symmetry and proportion, with serious consequences if the failure to conform persists.[1] In this respect there is evidence to show that the introduction of modern scientific methods had of late years increased the output of a number of important primary commodities to an extent which represented relative over-production, and, therefore, caused a more marked fall in prices than that revealed by the general downward tendency. This situation, it may be remarked in passing, is in strong contrast to the expectations in bygone years of Malthus and of Jevons. The former believed that the world's population imminently threatened to outgrow the increase in the means of subsistence. Jevons thought the British coal industry was in danger of suffering from early and dangerous depletion of the mines. It was believed that the force of these views would be amply demonstrated before the present epoch. It must be admitted, however, that Malthus, if he could return to Earth, might reasonably point to the present situation in Japan as illustrating some underlying basis of truth in his contention.

[1] The monetary aspect is examined in the ensuing chapter, "Monetary Chaos and the Fall in the Price Level."

The commodity position seems to be most accurately expressed by saying that, in the year or two preceding the slump, there was evidence of an incipient instability in the production of a number of foodstuffs and raw materials occupying an important place in the world's economic structure.

This mal-adjustment would not in itself have produced the crisis, but would in all probability have led to a depression similar in character to many of the countless periodic depressions that have recurred throughout the world's history.

It only awaited some untoward event to reveal the facts; and this event might itself set up forces to magnify the discrepancy.

In 1928 and early 1929 there was a downward tendency of commodity prices, and though it was slight and irregular, it occurred when the volume of trade was increasing. It was not till the Stock Exchange slump occurred in the autumn of 1929 that the commodity decline took definite shape and brought to view the weakness existing in certain places.

The evidence therefore points strongly to the fact that, apart from a catastrophic slump, the price of many commodities would have materially declined in recent years. The most conspicuous example of over-production occurred in the case of the rubber industry, where the price fell from a high peak of 4s. 8d. per lb. in 1924 to a low level of 1¾d. per lb. in May 1932. The sharp rise in price in 1925 was due to a sudden shortage following upon the enormous increase in automobile production in the United States. The profits of the producing companies expanded tremendously, and led to a great increase in the acreage cultivated by both the European publicly owned companies and by the native hand-to-mouth producer. A large number of new companies were floated, though many of these merely represented a change of ownership at the higher prices the estates commanded. This sudden outstanding prosperity was, however, a great injury to the permanent well-being of the industry. The increase in supply, even in the year 1925, proved to be adequate, and stocks have grown and the price fallen almost without a break ever since, except for the readjustment of the sterling price on our departure from the Gold Standard. In the rubber industry it has proved particularly difficult to curtail supply to the amount demanded. Trees once planted cannot be tapped for five years, and attempts at restriction have been frustrated by the existence of the native producer as an important element in supply, accustomed to a low standard of life and able to sell at a price which threatens the existence of the Company-owned estate. The latter are now engaged in " bud-grafting," rotational tapping, etc., in order to obtain a higher yield and lower average cost, but at the expense of increasing the total output. It is difficult to foresee the eventual outcome.

Coffee is another instance of clear over-production.

Brazil adopted the unfortunate expedient of "a defence scheme," the "defence" being that of the price by means of purchasing stocks in bulk and selling according to the conditions of the market. Unfortunately the money employed to purchase the stocks and operate the plan was not contributed by the coffee-grower but by the foreigner in the shape of public loans. The Government, moreover, encouraged the planting of a considerable new area; and since world output, apart from Brazil, was also growing rapidly and the price was maintained at an uneconomic level, a heavy drop was bound to have occurred earlier rather than later. The price in 1929–30 was less than one-third of that in 1926–27. Brazil is now using coffee treated with tar to drive railway trains, which may subsequently prove to mean good business for locomotive builders.

A situation somewhat similar in character to that of coffee has developed in the Sugar industry. The European countries have subsidized the sugar-beet, so that cultivation takes place at an uneconomic price in order to provide employment for their population and to alleviate the distress of the agricultural community generally. Producers of cane-sugar during the same time have substantially increased their output, chiefly as the result of an improvement in methods. The competition with the bounty-fed sugar has, nevertheless, proved severe and stocks have mounted almost uninterruptedly for many years.

Illustrations of the same tendency could be given in respect of Paper Pulp, an important industry in Canada, the United States and Scandinavia. In the case of Copper, both supply and demand had increased rapidly, but in 1929 supply was showing clear indications of overtaking demand, while copper areas of rich content in Rhodesia and other parts were being developed for production. An examination of the position of Lead, Zinc and Tin leads to conclusions of the same general character. Nitrate provides an instance of competition with another source of supply made possible by the chemist, as in the case of sugar. The market has so far not proved equal to taking both the synthetic and the natural article.

The most interesting case, however, is that of Wheat, the world's staple commodity. The chemist with his fertilizers, the biologist by segregating special resistant qualities for particular climates and soils, and, above all, the engineer with his agricultural machinery—especially the tractor and the combine—have all contributed their quota to a development as significant in its way as the coming of the railway train and steamship, which opened the great grain-growing countries to the European market. The revolution in methods wrought by the tractor is not generally realized in urban communities. It has ushered in the era of power-farming, affording employment to a smaller number of persons, but with an increase in individual output. The number of tractors employed has increased by leaps and bounds.

Mr. R. R. Enfield, in a valuable review of the position read before the British Association in 1931, gave particulars of the number manufactured in the United States of America. There was an increase from 60,000 in 1917 to about 229,000 in 1929. Another authority (Economic Section of the League of Nations) gives figures relating to the extended use of the combined Reaper and Thresher. During 1923–29, 68,000 were sold, of which two-thirds of the sales were made in 1928–29. The results of power-farming shown in reduced costs, diminished man-power, enlarged farms, cultivation of low-yielding areas, were only just becoming manifest before the financial storm broke.

Changes on the demand side have also been of a significant character. The rate of increase of population in the wheat-eating countries has slowed down considerably, and the consumption per head has shown a definite tendency to decline. Further, the animal labour previously employed where tractors are now used, accounted for some if only a small percentage of consumption. Moreover, the areas retained for raising crops for animal food are now set free for producing crops for human consumption. Nevertheless, the total of world consumption has increased in post-War years, though at a diminished rate. The International Institute of Agriculture estimated that consumption advanced from 764 million quintals as an average for the years 1909–13 to 828 million quintals as an average for 1925–29.

Therefore, despite the significance of the changes in the industry, stability might well have been maintained but for the unfortunate policy of laying down increased acreage which on the average of the years 1927–30 (excluding China and Russia) was over 22 per cent above that of the average for 1909–13.

The harvesting of a bumper crop in 1928, leading to a large carry-over to the next year, resulted in no violent fall, though, ever since the middle of 1924, there had been a drooping tendency rather more marked than that of wholesale prices generally.

It was the stock-market crash, and the failure of the attempt made by the Canadian Wheat Pool and the American Farm Board to keep prices near to the then existing level in spite of huge stocks and world depression, that led to a collapse. This attempt to sustain prices was made against the whole trend of the situation, for it was impossible to resist the conclusion that the market was ripe for a fall; this quite apart from external events which made it certain, and brought the price down to a little over a dollar a bushel at the end of 1930, compared with over two dollars in 1924. Since this heavy fall has occurred, all the great grain-growing countries outside Russia have materially contracted their acreage sown to wheat, and, while there is likely to be a surplus over requirements it is hoped that it will be smaller than for several years past. With Russia, different considerations have led to a considerable increase in acreage put down to wheat. Ten million additional acres was the original programme for 1931, though it is understood this was not reached. A further ten-million-acre increase is scheduled for 1932. That country was an important factor in the market before the War, and her re-entry in September 1930 was the cause of a sharp fall. For the whole year 1930 her exports were only 94 million bushels, compared with a world export of 1,132 million bushels. Of late she has been a purchaser; but nevertheless, it may be expected that her share of the export market will grow, in view of the steady expansion of the area cultivated and the rapid advance in the use of tractors and other agricultural machines.

Meanwhile the situation of those European countries, such as France and Germany, which have maintained the comparatively small wheat-farming units operated by the older methods, appears to be highly artificial. The cost of production is vastly greater than that of the wide areas cultivated by modern methods. Accordingly it has been necessary to support prices by huge import duties, so that the disparity in prices is remarkable, as the figures below indicate:

Prices, April 20, 1932. For quarters of 480 lb., and for month of May trading:

	s.	d.
Liverpool Futures	24	11
London Manitoba Futures	27	3
Paris Market Futures	78	3
Berlin Market Futures	74	10½

THE FUNDAMENTAL CAUSES OF THE WORLD SLUMP

Surveying the ground covered, it will be agreed that enough evidence has been adduced to show that the world had its difficulties to meet, apart from the special financial and monetary factors which finally not only overthrew the already precarious balance but made the fall so much heavier.

The proceeds of the sale of wheat constitute the predominant or a substantial proportion of the incomes of the people of Canada, Argentine, Australia and America, and of other small producers. Brazil is closely bound up with the fortunes of Coffee, Malaya with Rubber and Tin, the West Indies with Sugar, and so on. Accordingly the fall in prices reacted severely upon them all.

An increased natural return to the agents of production is, of course, beneficent in itself, and a fall in price does not necessarily indicate over-production or result in losses to the producer, since the decline may be generalized by an all-round increase in the efficiency of production. It might seem to some foolish that a more liberal return to the efforts of producers should be inimical to well-being. Nature and progress, it will be argued, have combined to increase the yield to labour and capital, which is the object of all enterprise. The gain to the producer should spread outward to the purchaser, who may reasonably expect to fulfil his requirements more cheaply. From the point of view of the creditor country there is a double advantage, since the capital loaned by these countries not only earns interest but, in so far as it has enabled needed goods to be obtained more cheaply, is receiving an additional return.

All this is true enough. The immediate point, however, is this: the prime necessity for the producer is to cover his total costs. Ability to do so depends on the movement in the price-level of the product. If downward, the occasion may arise when he is compelled to sell his goods whether costs are covered or not. Under no system of production can there be any sense in selling output for less than the cost of production. Under a capitalist system it is fatal. It changes prosperity to depression and the vicious circle is started. If the position is bad enough, as in the past few years, monetary factors may create further dislocation. The depression may damage the countries' credit to such an extent that at a time when new purchasing power is most needed further loans are denied. The producing country undergoes a serious contraction of business and employment. Where previously the sale price of exports was adequate to cover interest on loans and the purchase price of imports, the new situation may compel default on interest and a severe curtailment of imports. The creditor country is thus a loser in two directions, which together certainly outweigh the advantage of cheaper imports. This is, of course, not a merely hypothetical state of affairs, but the actual sequence of events in Brazil, Chili and elsewhere, and that which has threatened India, Australia and many other countries.

THE FUNDAMENTAL CAUSES OF THE WORLD SLUMP

Summing up, the commodity position would in any event have caused a depression. The crisis was caused by monetary and financial factors which will now be examined.

FAILURE TO OBSERVE THE CONDITIONS NECESSARY FOR THE SUCCESSFUL FUNCTIONING OF THE INTERNATIONAL GOLD STANDARD

Before the War responsibility for the smooth operation of the system of international exchange devolved mainly upon Great Britain. She was by far the most important country in the sphere of world trade and finance, and over a long period of years had become habituated to the measures necessary to enable the gold standard to perform its function. The primary and, indeed, obvious feature governing international trading relationships is the fact that stocks of gold constitute only a very small fraction of the value of goods and services traded between one country and another. Consequently the art of manipulating the gold standard is to maximize the extent to which payments due are settled by the exchange of goods and to minimize the passage of gold.

Great Britain achieved this object successfully. She was the greatest exporter of goods and placed no obstacle in the way of overseas countries sending goods in return. The universality of her exports enabled her to develop the bill of exchange system. Since every country sold to her and every country bought from her, the overseas produce merchant who had sold goods to Britain could readily sell his sterling bill of exchange to the man next door, or in another country, who had bought British goods for which he wished to pay. The sterling bill based on goods was the world's accepted medium of settlement. In consequence its position provided the foundation for the growth of the banking, bill broking, insurance, stock-exchange and general finance business. Thus in the financial sphere a predominance without serious rival was achieved; while the actual carriage of goods was responsible for our maritime supremacy. (Let us remember these facts before speaking too glibly of the foolishness of Free Trade.)

The profits on these ancillary services, as well as the terms of trade in actual goods (buying primary commodities and selling made-up), led to a steady increase in the balance of payments due to us from the outside world, a balance which obviously could not for long have been met by shipments of gold, and which by established policy was consistently invested abroad in the shape of long-term capital loans, the interest on which formed another invisible export.

The actual passage of gold, therefore, formed an insignificant proportion of the total trade transactions.

From the situation which this country thus occupied it is easy to understand that Great Britain became the controlling influence, and therefore the market, for the world's gold stock. London drew gold from abroad, however, only in cases of sudden emergency such as a failure of crops where it covered a deficiency in payments (except in the case of countries engaged in gold-mining, such as South Africa, where the metal enters normally into international trade as a product of industry). On the other hand, this country seldom was called upon to part with much gold, since, whenever the trend was towards an efflux, all she required to do was to allow a small proportion of her acceptances[1] to "run off" in order to turn the balance of payments again in her favour. Moreover, the beginning of an outflow served both as a warning and a corrective. The loss of gold led to a restriction of the credit facilities based on gold; the Bank Rate, and therefore the general rate of interest, was accordingly raised, which tended to the reduction of foreign acceptances and encouraged foreign money to enter in order to earn the higher rate of interest.

The financial effects of the loss of gold were reinforced by its further influences on the flow of international trade in goods. The depreciation of the Exchange Rate which led to the outflow in itself cheapened home goods to the foreign buyer, while internally the contraction of credit would tend to change the market sentiment of traders, making the seller more eager to conclude the bargain and the buyer less so. The domestic price level

[1] Engagements to pay bills of exchange on behalf of another, chiefly on account of foreign trade, and therefore in effect short-term loans secured upon goods.

would thus be reduced and offer further inducements to the foreign purchaser. In the case of the country receiving gold the process would be exactly reversed, in effect duplicating the corrective sequence.

It is necessary to recall these facts, however well known they may be to some, in order to show that in recent years circumstances have combined to throw some of these most important components of this intricate machine out of gear. The whole succession of correctives has therefore been partially inoperative.

It has been shown that before the War Great Britain was mainly responsible for the functioning of the international Gold Standard. She herself may not have been fully conscious of the importance of the role she performed; in any case it seems certain that its significance was not fully appreciated abroad. Thus a new position was created when, after Great Britain's return to gold in 1925, she found that responsibility for working the Gold Standard was henceforth to be shared with others, who did not necessarily accept as a guide the methods and principles of former years. The difficulty of the situation was increased by the fact that the various countries of the world were mostly preoccupied with their individual aspirations and intended to make economic considerations subservient to political purposes.

THE FUNDAMENTAL CAUSES OF THE WORLD SLUMP

The economic practices of the present day are thus partly a legacy of the War, which promoted a wave of intense nationalistic feeling. The influence of this emotion has been carried into the trade sphere and has resulted in a stultifying policy bound from the first to recoil, as it has, with penalties upon guilty and innocent alike. The idea has been to buy less and less from other countries while endeavouring to sell them more. Obviously the actual outcome, a contraction of trade due not only to exclusion by tariffs, but in its later stages by lack of bills of exchange to effect payment, was foredoomed from the start. Moreover, the intense concentration upon an export surplus was bound to constrain free-trade and semi-free-trade countries to revert to a protectionist system—a retrograde step in the corporate interest.

Deplorable as this exaggerated nationalism has been in its effect upon normal trade in goods, it has been far worse in its repercussions on the previously accepted policy of overseas investment by which creditor countries —or those with the balance of international payments in their favour—lent their balances abroad in the shape of long-term capital issues and so kept goods circulating instead of drawing off gold with all its dislocating consequences.

The countries with whom Great Britain has been called upon to share her responsibilities in international finance are the United States of America and France.

The assertion can fairly be made that these two countries have traditionally manifested a reluctance towards lending abroad on a large scale. In the former country the investor has regarded more favourably the opportunity for the profitable employment of capital at home. In the latter country large-scale foreign investment tends to be linked to political consideration, an influence which does not favour the discharge of a purely economic function.

In the case of America, however, the vast growth of the indebtedness of the outside world which had already drawn off the bulk of the world's entire stock of gold almost compelled a series of long-term loans chiefly to Central and South America and Central Europe.

Commencing about 1924 this movement was much stimulated by the cheap-money policy instituted by the Federal Reserve Authority of the United States, with the express desire to help Europe with foreign loans and to repatriate some of America's superabundant stocks of metal. The desired effect was created. By 1928 long-term loans on foreign account totalled $4,789 million, about twice that of Great Britain in the same period. Gold flowed out from America towards the latter part of the period to the extent of $600 million.

Unfortunately for the good intentions of the banking authorities of America about 1928 the incipient stock-market boom in that country was gathering force. The

THE FUNDAMENTAL CAUSES OF THE WORLD SLUMP

endeavour to check this movement caused a reversal of the cheap-money policy, and ultimately not only led to a complete cessation of capital flotations on behalf of external borrowers, but actually caused capital, some hundreds of millions of dollars being in gold, to flow from Europe to America in order to earn the high rates offered in the later stages of the boom.

The net result was only to leave the borrowing nations worse off than before. The purchasing power acquired had encouraged expansive schemes, which subsequently became a liability to be upheld in addition to interest charges on the borrowed money—and this at a time when normal income was greatly reduced.

The last blow to the effective working of the international gold standard has been dealt by the curtailment of its function to act as an automatic corrective to divergent price levels. Largely this has been due to the preceding conditions and to the weight of gold movements. Incoming gold has been to some extent "sterilized" (at any rate in France); that is it has not been allowed to serve as a basis for an expansion of credit with its corollaries in raising internal prices and attracting foreign imports.

In self-defence countries losing gold have to some extent prevented the loss exercising its full normal effect. The means adopted has been for the Central Bank to purchase bills or securities in the market which has the effect of providing their Member banks with a balance at the Central Bank—say the Bank of England—which ranks as cash. In this way the full effect of the loss of gold is diminished. Gold treated in this way is said to be "offset."

This is but the briefest recapitulation of some of the chief differences between the pre-War and post-War methods of operating the gold standard.

Sufficient has been said, however, to show that before the War there was a conscious effort to observe the fundamental principles necessary for the functioning of the system. Since the War it is impossible to distinguish any coherent international policy. Complete financial breakdown has been staved off only by reason of the inherent resilience and resistant powers of the modern banking system.

REPARATIONS AND INTER-ALLIED WAR DEBTS

The powerful influence of this special factor in causing the financial breakdown has already received such widespread attention that it will be possible to dismiss the subject with more brevity than its importance would otherwise permit.

The attitude that has marked the handling of the whole question of Reparations and Inter-Allied War Debts is in part an outstanding but by no means isolated manifestation of the inconsistent economic nationalism

THE FUNDAMENTAL CAUSES OF THE WORLD SLUMP

which has just been described. The obligations involved can in the long run be discharged by an export surplus of goods (or their equivalent in services) and by that only, whatever financial jugglery takes place in the interim. The attitude of the creditor countries, however, has amounted to this: "Sell your goods elsewhere, but send the money to us." The effort of the debtor to fight a way into foreign markets has, of necessity, taken the form of an intensive and damaging competition in which price cutting, wage cutting, state stimulation of exports in bounties open or disguised, have all played a part.

The history of the War debts is found to be an account of the successive abandonment of a number of demands or arrangements which have proved impossible to implement.

The subject was opened in an atmosphere of unreality. Many will remember the speech of M. Klotz, the French Minister of Finance[1]—who informed the Chamber of Deputies that the allied claims against Germany amounted to £15,000 million, which would accumulate at interest till 1921 and be paid off thereafter by thirty-four annual instalments of about £1,000 million, of which France would receive rather more than half.

It was not the views of M. Klotz that were important. This gentleman subsequently demonstrated his unreliability in financial matters in other ways. But signi-

[1] Referred to by Mr. J. M. Keynes in his *Economic Consequences of the Peace*.

ficance attaches to the speech as being a good example of many that were made on both sides of the Channel, arousing hopes and expectations in the public mind which were only slowly and reluctantly relinquished. This particular speech was favourably received in political and financial circles and led to a cheerful sentiment on the Bourse accompanied by a rise in quotations.

The Treaty of Versailles established as a principle the liability of Germany to make reparation for "all loss and damage" to which the Allied Powers had been subjected, but recognized that it might not prove possible for Germany to pay. After various schemes and proposals had been mooted a Reparations Commission was appointed which met in 1921. This body reduced the total claim mentioned in 1920 (at the Boulogne Conference) by more than half, but put forward a plan designed to collect 132,000 million gold marks—say sixty-six thousand million pounds. The scheme of payments included a demand for 1,000 million gold marks in cash by September 1921. The attempt to meet this requirement was directly responsible for the decline in the exchange value of the mark, which ended in a complete collapse of the currency, and so led to the extinction of individual savings where these were represented by fixed-interest obligations and cash deposits: and while industry was thereby relieved of debt obligations it was also entirely denuded of working capital.

The Dawes Plan in 1924, in its turn, halved the amount

of the annuities immediately payable, by a reduction from 2,000 million gold marks to 1,000 million, but it established a schedule of rising annual payments reaching 2,500 million gold marks for 1928–29. This was more than the 1921 figures of 2,000 million, but dropped the additional 26 per cent of German exports. The Dawes Scheme further provided for the flotation of a loan to enable Germany's demoralized currency system to be sufficiently re-established to make payment of foreign exchange practicable. The lending of money to an ex-enemy country was thought by many irreconcilables to be a deplorable act. They were blind to the fact that far from being prompted by any philanthropic motive the loan was designed to make the debt collection possible. The difficulties of operating the Dawes scheme, particularly the responsibility thrown upon the creditor countries of receiving the money in Germany and of transferring the vast sums involved from marks into the currency of the recipient countries, led to the appointment of a further body, from which emerged the Young Plan of 1929. By the new scheme the task of transfer was thrown upon Germany as a *quid pro quo* for "taking the brokers out." The annuities were further reduced, the first payment being fixed at 1707·9 million marks for 1930—the first full year of operation. The scheme also provided for the raising by public subscription in various countries of another international loan to a total of $300 million. One third of this sum was to go to Germany to alleviate the capital famine there by which the most impossible rates of interest for loans were being charged, even to first-class houses. The other two thirds were to be divided among the creditor countries.

The procedure to be adopted in raising the new public loan was the subject of somewhat prolonged differences between this country and France. These were mainly due to our refusal to agree to the portion of the loan floated in London being for a larger capital sum than we were to receive as our share of the total proceeds. We further refused to allow the loans raised abroad to be interchangeable with that raised here. Had it been otherwise foreign portions of the loan would have been saleable in London from foreign houses: a very probable result as experience has taught us. Our objection, of course, was dictated by the need of preventing the London Stock Exchange becoming as vulnerable to French sales as the banking system already was to French withdrawals. In both cases the ultimate reaction would be upon the sterling exchange.

The chief merit of the Young Plan was the establishment of the Bank of International Settlements, which was appointed to receive and allocate the payments transferred by Germany. The Bank formed a close link with the chief central banks of the world and its periodic meetings induced a measure of co-operation, which it may be hoped will increase in the future. The Young scheme also possessed the merit of recognizing the possibility of Germany's being unable to transfer the full amount stipulated, and, accordingly, divided the annuities into two parts:

(1) The Unconditional portion, being a sum of RM. 660 million.

(2) The remainder, which was conditional upon the ability to transfer the sums due into foreign currency. If Germany regarded herself as unable to obtain foreign exchange to the required amount, she was given the right to invoke the sanction of the Bank of International Settlements to a two years' postponement.

The proportions of the unconditional annuity to be allocated to each of the creditor countries led to further acute differences between this country and France. The strong stand made by Mr. Snowden (as he then was) will be within the recollection of most.

The Young Plan, however, was an ailing infant from birth. A mistake was made in removing the "purchasing power of gold" clauses which attached to the Dawes Plan and took the shape of a relationship between the amounts payable by Germany and the general price-level. The Young Committee met in the early part of 1929, and the aim of the Plan was to take the whole subject out of the sphere of politics and to submit it to a lasting and final settlement. Before the year was out the great Stock Exchange slump had ushered in the world depression with the effect of making the annuities grow steadily larger in terms of commodity values;

and this at a time when turn-over and profit-margins were dwindling at an alarming rate. The earning capacity of industry was thus entirely swamped by the demands made upon it. How was the purchase of foreign exchange to be undertaken under such conditions? The most obvious means by which foreign currency might have been made available was by the intermediary of a further long-term public loan, thus setting up a stream of payment in the opposite direction. Such a solution was rendered both impracticable and inadvisable by the existing circumstances. The only possible, though dangerous, alternative was that adopted, namely, to offer high rates of interest for short-term bank loans. Finance houses and bankers in other countries finding difficulty in employing their funds remuneratively were tempted to lend for periods of a few months at high remuneration. They counted on ability to withdraw if the situation appeared to be worsening. It seemed to be overlooked that an event of a threatening character would lead to such a rush of withdrawals as would inevitably cause a breakdown.

The endeavour to prevent a breakdown of this character was the underlying motive of the one-year moratorium announced by Mr. Hoover in June 1931. The proposal was hailed with great rejoicing at the time as foreshadowing the opening of a new and better era in international relationships. Hopes were soon dissipated, however, when it became clear that France was in two minds about accepting the proposal. There was a disquieting delay during which a movement to withdraw funds from Central Europe on the part of those who recognized the instability of the position gathered force. The disclosure of pending insolvency came from Austria, where the Government admitted that an important bank, the Credit Anstalt, would be unable to continue much longer. Negotiations were instantly set up by the Bank of England with a view to providing assistance in conjunction with others in order to avoid the inevitable repercussions which would precipitate a run on the banks and a probable financial cataclysm.

The Bank of France, while willing to lend the recognized proportion, insisted that political stipulations, notably the abandonment of the Austro-German Customs Union, should be attached to the loan. This Austria refused, and the Bank of England, dreading the results of further delay, advanced the whole sum, to the great annoyance of the French.

The knowledge of these differences further awakened the fears of all creditors of the Central Powers. A hurried scramble to withdraw from Germany and Austria ultimately widened to include this country, and led to our abandonment of the Gold Standard under circumstances that will be described later.

In November, Germany notified the Bank of International Settlements of its inability to continue the payments called for by the Young Plan. The Bank of

International Settlements appointed a Committee of Bankers representing each of the creditor countries to examine the position. The Committee was unanimous in reporting that Germany's balance of payments, including the export surplus, foreign assets, and credits obtained during the year, would be inadequate to enable her to transfer the conditional part of the annuity. This was all they were strictly entitled to report upon, but the implication was clear that neither could the unconditional annuity be met. They added a warning that the German problem, as being largely responsible for the growing financial paralysis of the world, called for early and concerted action by the countries concerned.

At the time of writing the meeting of yet another Conference to further consider the Reparations problem anew is being awaited. Perhaps a few comments may be offered here of some inevitable considerations that any further survey demands.

(1) The disorganizing effects of attempts to force transfers of funds beyond that which the margins of normal trade permit produce most damaging reactions on the foreign exchange system and thence upon the credit structure.

(2) Heavy transfers in any case constitute a serious impediment to trade. The recipient countries are compelled to bear the brunt of intensified competition. Moreover, statistics show that the German export surplus in the critical years has been chiefly built up by

diminished imports implying a lower standard of life for the paying nations and a decline in the sales made to her by other nations.

(3) War debt and reparation payments are unlike normal interest payments in that the sums represented have no equivalence in the earning capacity of capital originally advanced.

(4) A heavy price has been paid for the serious divergence in policy between the central banks of England and France. The damage so wrought stands out in clear contrast to the happy results attending co-operative effort, as on the occasion of the financial reconstructions of Austria and Hungary in the early post-War years under the auspices of the League of Nations.

The disharmony which has been introduced by the Reparations issue has, of course, roots that lie far deeper than differences on financial policy.

France has twice been invaded within the span of a normal lifetime. Invasion and the near-by devastation of the homes of the people produce a powerful psychological revulsion which must awaken comprehension and sympathy in this country. For France it means that the dynamic force behind her aims is a passionate belief in the justice of her cause.

The Englishman for his part is anxious to see fair play for France, but holds it foolish to fly in the face of the hurtful economic reactions. And reinforcing his viewpoint is an emotion he is generally too shy to express:

"Would it not be better to let bygones be bygones and try to build on a better foundation?" The higher morality is strangely in accord with the sounder practical policy.

(5) Great Britain stands for complete cancellation. France and America are opposed to this course. So much for policy. What are the indisputable facts? That in any near term Germany will be unable to pay on a substantial scale. It is unthinkable that ex-ally debts should be accorded less favourable treatment than ex-enemy debts. It is equally unthinkable that Great Britain can be left to continue her payments indefinitely in "splendid isolation."

THE WALL STREET CRASH [1]

The Wall Street boom of 1928–29 was the greatest stock-market boom in history and was followed by the biggest crash. In its early stages it was based on a solid grounding of prosperity. Rich endowments in natural resources were ready to the hand of a people gifted with great qualities of business insight, imagination and organizing ability. The mechanistic trend of the post-War era was exactly suited to the American temperament, while

[1] In regard to what is to follow let it be said at once that every stock exchange in the world participated in the boom, and in the slump that followed. The craze to "get rich quick" was not confined to any one country. But the range of price fluctuations, the numbers engaged, weight of capital involved, and the extent to which other stock exchanges were carried on the tide of Wall Street, all demand that attention be concentrated on this centre.

their extensive self-contained internal market offered exceptional advantages for the initial stages of development. From the first, therefore, America was the protagonist of mass production methods, scientific lay-out, intensive application of power drive, carefully planned marketing schemes, psychology of salesmanship and so on. In 1922, after the universal depression of the previous year, trade in America showed an improving tendency. This is what the Federal Reserve Banking Authorities were waiting for in order to foster the movement by a liberal credit policy. A policy of credit expansion was for them comparatively unadventurous owing to the enormous accumulation of gold stocks which occurred during and after the War; but it was subsequently maintained with consistency, whether gold movements were inward or outward. In 1925 and 1926 the trade improvement became pronounced. In both these years stock-market quotations moved upward, and this was followed by a further substantial rise in 1927. As a consequence the share-market aspect of the situation absorbed an increasing amount of attention. Naturally the increased profits earned by the successful industries mainly accrued to the holder of the equity or Common stocks, since the amount required for prior charges was generally not much greater, leaving the residual earnings available for the Common stock-holder. The extent of the movement in share values will readily be gleaned by reference to the price range of a number of popular and representative shares for the years 1926, 1927 and 1928. (*Vide* Appendix.)

Profits on this scale reaped by holders of a wide range of Common stocks whetted the appetites of the participants and excited the envy of spectators. The field began to widen, and before 1928 was far advanced boom-time conditions ruled. All sorts of people, workmen, tradesmen, men outside the business world, who had no previous experience of stock-exchange technique, were coming in to take a hand. Many women became ardent and active speculators. They expected to be told how they could make money without having to wait for results. A lady of this type would call upon her broker and explain that she sought advice in regard to investments. A few high-grade safety-first fixed-interest-bearing stocks would be suggested. The lady murmuring her thanks would depart seeking the advice of a more live and imaginative financial guide. A number of men set to work on money-making "systems." As the system generally amounted to deciding the purchase of leading shares after so many points fall, and the general trend of the market was upward, the system operators were mostly successful, felt themselves to be very clever fellows and told their friends about it. Every day brought a larger public into the market and bigger orders. People were able to send larger orders by borrowing on margin. Great confidence in the future was the prevailing sentiment, and as long as the current price of the stock purchased exceeded the amount borrowed by a substantial percentage, bankers and brokers were willing to advance loans against purchase. Moreover, the sum borrowed was almost always subject to "call" at short notice, so that little risk was run by the lender. The amount so borrowed, and therefore used entirely for speculative purposes, steadily increased. In the latter part of 1928 it rose for fifteen consecutive weeks without a set-back to a total of well over five billion dollars, and at the end of the time represented an expansion of more than one-and-a-half billion dollars since the beginning of the year. The banks endeavoured to check this movement, realizing the danger to the financial structure of the world. It has already been mentioned that up to the middle of 1928 America had been lending capital freely to Europe and South America. She had, in fact, become by far the world's most important exporter of capital. The financial authorities perceived that the speculative fever by monopolizing the attention of the public would divert interest from all attempts to raise fixed-interest loans for foreign countries and leave the latter seriously embarrassed. They were right. In the second half of 1928 new loans for Europe fell to negligible dimensions and were not again resumed. But the attempt to check the tendency by raising money rates was not logically pressed home. The step taken simply meant increasing the remuneration to those who lent money for speculation. To a public eager to borrow and making quick profits in a few days an addition of one or two, or three or four, per cent per annum made little difference. Unfortunately many financial houses in Europe, finding it difficult to employ their money remuneratively at home, or to find some long-term investments, were attracted by a high rate of interest offered "for call" and sent large sums to New York, so that the flow of funds was actually reversed.

The rising share prices which enriched the public encouraged free and open-handed expenditure, which in turn was reflected in the earnings of the industry and provided the basis for further rises in the share market. The individual in his private capacity spent liberally; in his capacity of business chief or public man the same attitude of mind was reflected in enlargements and improvements. It was hard for the individual to prevent expenditure overlapping income account into that of capital. Imagine Mr. Babbitt urged by his family to provide them with a new car. He has previously refused. But the next day on his way home from business he reads in the evening paper that Montgomery Ward have risen ten points, and is thereupon persuaded. Mr. McKelvey, in a much bigger way of business, is similarly actuated. When as president of a large corporation the past quarter's sales figures are put before him, he decides to proceed immediately with the scheme he has been contemplating for some time, remodelling the factory and increasing output by 20 per cent.

THE FUNDAMENTAL CAUSES OF THE WORLD SLUMP

The year 1928 closed with the country simply abounding in prosperity. While England was hopefully striving for the day when her tragic army of unemployed might number less than a million, and doubtful whether the subsistence level were not too high to prevent absorption, American artisans were going to their jobs in cars, so that near any big edifice under construction was a park of automobiles suggestive of a race meeting.

Most of the prophets faced the new year with confident expectation. "No complaint of the level of stock prices is justified except from the point of credit strain," wrote one. "It is only when current savings are inadequate to keep pace with advance of prices and huge borrowing for carriage of stocks brings a competition with business for the always limited supply of lendable funds that danger appears." There is only a vague fear here of possible unsound credit conditions. Looking back it seems curious that all well-informed people did not realize that the whole movement was only sustained by rising prices. Yet confident expressions were the rule and emanated from the lips of business men, administrators and economists of the highest repute.

The voice of warning was not lacking, however. Faced with a tabulation showing brokers' loans at December 31, 1928, to be nearly $6\frac{1}{2}$ billion dollars (say one-and-a-quarter thousand million pounds) and representing plain borrowing for speculation on margin, the editor of the *Financial and Commercial Chronicle* in his

New York leader wrote in these terms: "It is difficult for any well-informed commentator who has an appreciation of what figures of such magnitude as those contained therein mean—what a menace they involve to the entire community—to speak with restraint and in calm temperate language of the way the movement is proceeding week after week and month after month without the slightest suggestion the inevitable end is in sight or even nearer. It is impossible to characterize such a situation without resort to expressions and terms which to the ordinary mind will seem extreme; and yet the situation merits the severest strictures and really makes it a public duty for anyone in authority or having influence or weight to speak in unsparing denunciation of what is going on."

For a considerable time it seemed that events sufficed to contradict this view. In fact, not a few of those who believed in an impending crash found their own authority weakened and confidence in their own predictions sapped by the contradiction of actual happenings. The earnings of many branches of industry for the first half of 1929 cast those of 1928 in the shade. Amusement companies up 77 per cent, automobile accessories 44 per cent, oil producing and refining 79 per cent. The average car output for 1925–28 was 4,000,000, that for 1928 itself being 4,358,000. Up to August 31, 1929, the rate of output was in excess of 6,000,000 per annum.

A report on the transport situation which was published about this time indicated that there were about 25,000,000 automobiles on the roads of America. It was suggested, however, that preparations should be made to receive an increase to 50,000,000 within a few years. The additional road construction, garage accommodation, service stations, gasoline pumps, retail and accessory stores required were then dealt with. Even these were small compared with the addition to the already enormous demands of the motor industry for steel, seasoned wood, plate glass, aluminium, nickel and so on, which would be set in motion.

With well-authenticated reports of this kind in their hands what wonder that the American public really believed they had solved an age-old problem and banished poverty. Indeed, an official body set up by Mr. Hoover to report on economic affairs practically told them so.

"While the appetite for goods and services is practically insatiable as it appears to be, and so long as productivity can be constantly increased, it would seem that we can go on with increasing activity" without cause for anxiety. These views were endorsed by publicists and economists of world-wide reputation. Another American writer, however, caustically observed that the current process was like trying to "finance a perpetual fireworks display for every family." In the end the necessary credit for effecting purchases must burn itself out, but in the meantime "may we not bankrupt the world?"

Meantime European financial centres were suffering a severe strain.

In the first nine months of 1929 the Bank of England lost £23 million of gold. Its stocks fell at the end of the period to £133·2 million. This figure is very close to the amount held by the Bank at the time of our departure from the gold standard in September 1931.

The drain came from other countries in Europe as well as America. Call money was 10 per cent; no wonder people were not content to leave it at home to earn under 5 per cent or less. All Europe was sending funds to America and gold was again flowing outward—to the extent of $282 million in nine months.

About this time a gentleman named Mr. Clarence C. Hatry walked into the office of the Public Prosecutor and announced that he and his associates had committed grave irregularities in conducting the finances of their group of companies. Dealings were suspended on the Stock Exchange in the shares of seven of the companies concerned. The directors of the Bank raised the bank-rate to 6½ per cent—a step decided upon apart from the Hatry affair. A very unpleasant atmosphere was created. Heavy falls—or what were then thought to be heavy falls—occurred on every stock exchange in the world.[1] Leading shares in Wall Street fell five, ten and fifteen points. In the early part of October the Stock

[1] A London financial paper reported that all issues were weak except the Kylsant Shipping group, which had previously been "weak on the circulation of pessimistic rumours"!

Exchange compilations of brokers' loans[1] reached the record total of $8,549,383,000. At this time call money was 8 per cent or 10 per cent or more, and the average yield on industrial shares about 3 per cent.

In the middle of October a majority of shares had severe falls, but strangely enough many created new "highs." There were some who saw clearly enough what was about to happen. "Now the sad awakening has come whether the lesson it teaches has been learnt or not," wrote one. A day or two later the storm broke. Scenes beyond description and utterly without precedent occurred on the floor of the market. On Monday, October 28th, the shares recorded as sold on the Stock Exchange numbered over nine million, with a further four million odd on the Curb. On Tuesday even this astonishing total was completely outstripped with a combined total of $23\frac{1}{2}$ million shares. The total depreciations on these two days were estimated to involve an aggregate of $15,000,000,000 and $18,000,000,000 respectively. On the Monday General Electric fell $47\frac{1}{2}$ points with a further fall on Tuesday of 28 points. American Telegraph & Telephone fell 34 points and then 28 points, United States Steel $17\frac{1}{2}$ and 11, and so throughout the list, the only variation being the extent of the fall.

On the first signs of the outbreak of trouble lenders had called in their loans on a colossal scale. The bankers

[1] This compilation is more comprehensive than that of the Federal Reserve Authorities and therefore more accurately reflects the situation. The Federal Reserve figure was $6,804,000,000.

stepped in to a partial extent, but clearly could not take over completely. The unfinanced portion had to be sold for what it would fetch. Many heavily committed people, including large numbers who had utterly failed to realize the risks they were carrying, wandered about in a bewildered condition endeavouring to escape disaster, as they thought, by putting up fresh cover, in many cases pledging house and home and personal jewellery to avoid further sales. Better for them if they had faced the facts and cut their losses outright. But the lesson was still not learnt. Many so-called prophets and experts declared it was all a mistake. Others saw it for what it was, for example, the *Financial and Commercial Chronicle* which had previously been so wise in its advice. The incredible thing is that on the two days following the great slump a tremendous recovery occurred to an extent which almost wiped out the previous losses. As a consequence the whole disillusioning process had to be gone over again. A series of panics overwhelmed the market in November. On one very black day, November 13th, prices were carried to much below those ruling on October 29th. At this time a huge order was placed in the market, believed to emanate from Mr. Rockefeller, to buy 1,000,000 Standard Oil of New Jersey at 50. This caused a rebound in this particular share and steadied the whole market for a time, only to be followed by further declines in succeeding weeks.

The last three months of 1929 had witnessed a depreciation in New York stock-market values estimated to amount to 26 billion dollars.

At the close of 1929 and beginning of 1930 American confidence reasserted itself. The political and industrial leaders made reassuring statements. Preparations were made to reorganize prosperity. Brokers' loans were already greatly diminished. The banks reduced interest rates, the Government reduced the taxes and many people felt that a fresh start was about to be made. The end of 1930, however, closed with a disillusionment far more complete than that of twelve months before. It was realized that just as a boom is said "to feed on its own meat" so in a slump prices are borne down by their own weight. Especially is this the case when a large amount of stock is held with the banks "on margin." When prices fall the margin of cover runs off, and if banks were content to retain the collateral security under such circumstances and in large blocks their solvency would be threatened. Consequently further sales are enforced and these in turn create fresh low levels. The lost margin, however, represented the original owners' capital interest in the stock, and their losses, according to their relative proportion, necessitated economies ranging from a mere restriction of luxury expenditure to serious deprivation and hardship. This sudden curtailment of consumption was, of course, reflected in diminished trade, increased unemployment and the whole series of economic maladies with which we are all too familiar. In 1929 it was thought that 50 represented a panic price for Standard Oil. This share fell to 26 in 1931 and yet showed much better resistance than most Common shares. The fall in Common shares spread in an alarming degree to bond values also. A number of the smaller banks, unable to realize their assets, failed, and this, while not threatening the stability of the banking system as a whole, thoroughly alarmed a public which had already suffered so heavily from stock depreciation. Financial scares lead business houses and individuals to make their guiding policy the attempt to "get liquid," which means to withdraw money from investment and hoard it or place it with banks of unquestionable solidity. Borrowers for long term are therefore called upon to pay an exorbitant rate of interest which makes the employment of additional capital the more impossible.

All the evil chain of circumstances described here as relating to the United States may be applied in principle the world over, the only difference being that of degree. An examination of the course of share prices in the various financial centres of the world reveals a fall in industrial shares by the middle of 1931 from the highest reached, approximating to 60 per cent in Germany, Netherlands and the United States of America, 55 per cent in the case of France, 45 per cent in the United Kingdom and 30 per cent in Sweden.[1]

[1] According to statistics compiled by the League of Nations Economic section the market value of all stocks quoted on the New York market

THE FUNDAMENTAL CAUSES OF THE WORLD SLUMP

The whole world was therefore carried into the vortex of the slump and, so far, has struggled in vain to set itself free. But though the after-effects of the experience have not disappeared, the stock-market situation is no longer in itself a deterrent to revival. Brokers' loans have long since been reduced to negligible dimensions, and the wave of sales due to uncovered margins has subsided. But since the state of trade is now the barometer no recovery has occurred. Its readings have certainly provided no source of encouragement. Prices have continued to fall to ever lower levels, those registered subsequently to the Kreuger collapse being the lowest reached since the slump commenced. The Standard Statistics Company compile an index of New York Stock Exchange values covering some hundreds of shares. Taking 1926 as the base at 100, the index reached a level of 189·4 as an average for 1929, and fell to 41·7 in April 1932.

was estimated in January 1927 at $38,376,000,000, in January 1929 at $67,478,000,000, at $89,668,000,000 in September 1929, $63,589,000,000 in December 1929, and $48,470,000,000 in May 1931.

CHAPTER II

MONETARY CHAOS AND THE FALL IN THE PRICE LEVEL

The world slump is sometimes regarded as being adequately explained when related to the fall in commodity prices. Such an explanation will not suffice, however, for two reasons. In the first place a general reduction in prices might be due simply to an all-round improvement in the arts of production by means of which a larger return follows a given expenditure of capital and effort, thus lowering the cost price per unit. To a considerable extent this factor has operated; for example, from the increased use of power and machinery. Modern efficiency methods have contributed to a similar result. Take as instances rationalization, or the concentration of output upon the most efficient producers; and standardization, or design to secure maximum output per unit of plant. The application of these modern innovations has tended to lower the price level of a wide range of goods. In this respect the tendency to lower prices might be regarded as the natural outcome of scientific development. Representing greater efficiency such methods have tended on the whole towards a higher standard of living. If these were the chief influences operating to reduce the price level there would be little cause for complaint. Unfortunately, however, the more fundamental causes have been far from salutary in nature. The other reason for demanding a further explanation of the cause of the slump is that a fall in the general price level is not a cause but an effect. In the case of the present world depression it is an effect related to circumstances already described: not directly related however, but through the intermediary of the monetary mechanism. In other words, "the general price level is a monetary phenomenon." It is an expression of the relationship between existing purchasing power (money and credit) and the goods and services offered for sale. Some authorities hold the opinion that it is unnecessary to go beyond the imperfections of the monetary mechanism to discover a sufficient explanation for the decline in the price level. This is tantamount to saying that the monetary system can be made capable of adjusting itself to every external disorder. Certainly such a view is far nearer the truth than the average man recognizes. The question is one that was considered by the Macmillan Committee. They found that their witnesses were divided into two groups, those who regarded the fall in prices as primarily due to monetary causes and those who thought otherwise. The Committee observed that to ascribe the fall in prices to changes and disturbances of a non-monetary character might not be inconsistent in diagnosis with the view that the fall in prices was due to failure of the monetary machine to adjust itself to such changes and disturbances.

Some would go further, however, and say that had the monetary machine been operated with greater knowledge and wisdom the fall in prices could have been avoided. This raises the question "At what stage of events are the monetary authorities assumed to be in control?" Are the monetary managers to be left to deal with an uneconomic policy thrust upon them? Or to endeavour to operate a policy at variance with that pursued in other quarters? If these, the actual conditions, be allowed, the only reasonable conclusion to be drawn is that monetary management alone was incapable of correcting external derangements and preventing the fall in the general price level.

Moreover, experience has shown that the monetary factor does not correct external maladjustment as readily as at one time was supposed. Take the case already mentioned of over-production of certain staple commodities. It is frequently argued that the monetary mechanism is adequate to correct any disequilibrium of this kind which may appear. The article in over-supply will fall in price, profits will diminish or disappear and production as a consequence be curtailed.

In practice, however, the sequence does not work out with such simple effectiveness. The farmer or rubber-grower who is threatened with extinction does not give up without a struggle. He endeavours to cut costs, to introduce improvements and in general to produce more cheaply. Cheaper production sometimes means production on a larger scale, which so far from acting as an immediate corrective makes matters worse for the time being, so that ultimate stability is only achieved after a long-drawn-out struggle, during which large and important groups of producers may reach actual insolvency, crippling not only themselves but the whole community in which they function. Instances already given show that this is far from being a merely hypothetical state of affairs. As a rule the attempt is made substantially to hold the previously current price as long as possible. If outer events prove too strong or the over-supply is too pronounced the restriction scheme breaks down, and the accumulated stocks have to be unloaded on an unwilling market, so that a serious break in prices occurs. Clearly, however, a relative superfluity of this nature would be exaggerated by the failure of industry as a whole to expand, and the most dire effects even in recent experience are more specifically related to general causes than might at first sight be realized. It will be freely admitted therefore, and is widely agreed, that the great world depression is, in the main, the outcome of abuses of the monetary system of various kinds. The manner in which these abuses have continued to drive down the price level to lower and ever lower levels, and the stresses which are thereby set up in the internal economic structure, require further consideration. Brief mention has already been made of the havoc wrought by the War in the currency systems of nearly every country in the world, the belligerents, as a rule, being especially severe sufferers. In the post-War reconstruction period successful efforts were made to restore the credit of the most damaged countries in order to enable their respective currencies again to be placed on a sound footing. Thus the League of Nations undertook the reconstruction of Austrian finances in 1922 and those of Hungary in 1924. The German currency, too, was stabilized in 1924 by means of the Dawes Loan. Sweden in that year reverted to gold on the same basis as before the War. Great Britain followed in 1925, also on the pre-War valuation. Her lead resulted in a number of other countries linking their currencies to the gold standard in various ratios of the previous parities. For several years longer, however, many important nations such as France, Belgium, Poland and several South American States were still involved in a fluctuating paper currency. It was not until the end of 1926, when France stabilized the franc, that the bulk of the world's population was again exchanging its goods in prices based on the value of gold. In this country the deciding consideration determining our return to gold on the pre-War parity was the fact that contracts entered into in the normal times before the War had been undertaken on a specific basis, the £ sterling being a coin or a certificate representing a coin containing 123·27447 grains of gold $\frac{11}{12}$ fine.

The decision to carry out all our engagements in

terms of a currency carrying the pre-War gold content, made it necessary to bring the general price level of British goods into proximate relationship with that of America as the predominant power among gold-standard countries. If it be not immediately clear why the decision taken involved this course, it will become so when it is remembered that the adoption of a gold standard in common means that the prices of goods thereupon become gold prices. An endeavour to maintain a price level much above that prevalent in other gold-standard countries would invite a large-scale importation of goods, while at the same time damming up the stream of exports. The resultant loss of gold would either compel an adjustment of the price level or the abandonment of the gold standard. Thus the establishment of a sufficient approximation to the world level to maintain a "both ways" trading relationship is implicit in a return to gold payments. The penalties of the process, however, are undoubtedly severe. Before our resumption of the gold standard in 1925, for example, a parcel of goods selling in America at, say, $500 with exchange at, say, $4·40, realized £114 sterling, but with exchange at about parity of 4·86 the sterling value was only £103. The belief was held by those who advised the reversion to gold that this disability would be speedily corrected by a rise in the world price level—a view which we know was not vindicated by the facts.

Had this been the worst and only trial the exporter

had to face, his position would doubtless have proved tolerable. But such was not the case. In some other countries a totally different policy from our own had been pursued. This group had not only avoided the depressing effects of reducing the home level of prices, but had stabilized their currencies on terms which gave them a competitive advantage in the markets of the world for reasons which are widely understood.[1]

As a consequence the exporter from a deflationist country found himself in a position where his sales brought him a smaller sum in domestic currency, but yet was compelled to meet on competitive terms those for whom the situation was reversed. Countries which, like ourselves, were deflationist, included Czecho-Slovakia, Sweden and Switzerland. Among the inflationist group were France, Hungary and Italy. Germany in turn has come under both categories, and in each case appears to have tested the potentialities to the full extent. The whole body of traders in the former group were, of course, compelled to strain every nerve to cut prices. The competition was particularly severe for those already over-expanded industries which were endeavouring to obtain enough business to pay over-head costs.

There is very little doubt that the maladjustment of internal costs to external prices involved by the opposing policies of inflation and deflation had never been fully

[1] Internal prices—wages and other costs—do not necessarily rise to an extent corresponding to the external depreciation of the currency. Cost of production is, therefore, cheapened relative to prices in the world market.

MONETARY CHAOS AND THE FALL IN THE PRICE LEVEL

corrected before the full force of the depression was experienced.

It was on this kind of a world that the War-debts and Reparations obligations were superimposed. The accomplishment of the task set demanded the creation of an export surplus in a world unwilling to admit foreign goods. The result was again a strenuous and exacting effort to lower costs in respect of materials, wages and execution in order to force an entrance. Competition in its worst aspect was thus unavoidable.

Some mitigation of these conditions was experienced in the earlier stages of the American boom. Confidence was stimulated, the turnover in goods increased and made loan operations possible, which obscured the underlying realities. But with the collapse of the boom the prices of goods of all kinds tumbled pell-mell. From this time onwards the subsequent developments were really inevitable. The further disastrous fall in prices struck at the foundations of credit, the reason for which will be apparent if the nature of its reactions on internal economic structure is examined.

INTERNAL REACTIONS

A change in the price level disguises an alteration in the terms of the compact between debtor and creditor. If the change is downward, the debtor is favoured. If upward, the creditor. The discouragement to new enterprise is obvious. Capital expenditure tends to be postponed in order to avoid immediate depreciation; stocks of commodities carried are reduced to the smallest dimensions for the same reason. The falling price level acts as a brake upon industry.

While fresh commitments tend to be reduced, the burden of existing debts is increased. The currency unit on the average buys more goods. And, the fall in prices being normally prejudicial to trade, the total product of goods will probably be actually smaller.

The recipient of the fixed income is in such cases being given a larger relative share from a smaller actual total. But the important point to emphasize is that the re-distribution has consequences of immensely greater importance than that of making one section of the community better off at the expense of another. The real significance lies in its effect upon the profit margin. Under the capitalist system, the incentive to continue or develop a business or industry is ability to earn a profit. If the profit margin is zero or a minus quantity, the business or industry sooner or later dies. If the profit margin increases, the stimulus to expansion attracts further capital and labour.

It is not a matter of whether the share taken by profits is increasing its relative proportion of the earnings of the entire community, as long as the actual share provides an adequate standard of inducement. A falling price level resulting from a substantial expansion in production might quite probably lead to a decline in the relative share of profits, while the actual amount of profits was increasing. This would spell increasing prosperity for the whole community. But a falling price level, accompanied by languishing trade, strikes at profits with double force. The profit margin, in itself contracted by the state of trade, is further diminished by the relatively heavier burden involved in a fixed-money payment.

The problem in one aspect (another aspect will be treated at a later stage) in such circumstances is to adjust the shares of the prior claimants to the proceeds of industry. These are people deriving income from fixed charges, such as Government loans, debentures and other prior charges on industry. There is also the cost of maintaining Government and Municipal services, including social services, paid for in the shape of rates and taxes (the latter not wholly a prior claim, but nevertheless a deduction from the residual margin). An even more important prior claim comes from the largest group, namely, the whole body of wage and salary earners. If it should happen that, in a time of great depression and falling prices, these claimants all insisted upon maintaining a monetary *status quo*, profits would disappear and become a minus quantity.

There is no reason in equity why any group should be gainers by the adversity of the community. The position of the rentier class is therefore at such a time invidious. They may be compelled to accept a reduction, as in Australia and Germany, even in breach of contract. But breach of contract, except in gravest emergency, has rightly and properly a severe reaction on credit which tends to defeat itself. After the stage where crisis lends a "scare" value to money, the reduction of the rentier's share in times of falling trade should be brought about by monetary policy, operating at first through a reduction in the short-term rate. Otherwise, it is part of the great monetary problem of controlling the purchasing power of the currency.

A contraction in profit earnings tends to reduce either rates of wages or the volume of employment, since it no longer pays to retain the services of as many men at the previously existing rate of pay. The men whose services it only just paid to retain before would, on a lower profit basis, be retained only at a loss if the same wages were maintained throughout. To use a technical term, the marginal wage rate is diminished, that is, the rate at which it just pays to employ the body of workers at its existing number, instead of one less. A theoretical conception but a valuable one. The inability of industry to offer employment at the socially accepted wage rate throws the burden of maintenance upon the State. The increased expenditure involved comes at a time when the yield of taxation is lower owing to reduced profits. (It is true that expenditure for other Government and Municipal services may be reduced somewhat, but it is not likely to be sufficient

MONETARY CHAOS AND THE FALL IN THE PRICE LEVEL

in amount to offset the increased cost of unemployment and public assistance allowances.) The net result, therefore, is that the scale of taxation is raised and again reduces the residual margin. The strain upon the system is thus palpable. The real burden of fixed charges is increased and the profit margin reduced. State expenditure is weighted with the cost of maintaining a growing army of unemployed, while the yield to taxation is diminished. There must obviously be a breaking-point.

Such considerations were present in the minds of the financial community as a consequence of the unprecedented and prolonged fall in the prices of all goods following the stock-market slump. The credit of the various countries came under critical examination. Certain of them were scheduled as danger areas and debarred normal long-term credit facilities. Most of the primary producing countries found themselves in this category. Already heavily burdened with debt, they were unable at the lower level of prices to offer adequate security for further accommodation. Having been accustomed to rely upon capital loans for progressive development, this change in their circumstances came as a serious embarrassment.

Their predicament was mild, however, compared to that of the countries in Central Europe, whose hopeless plight became growingly more obvious. In respect of all these countries the sheer inability of declining trade to carry the large-scale transfers of debt interest was reflected in a drain of gold from the debtor countries to their creditors.

These withdrawals were on a scale of great magnitude. Sir Henry Strakosch has estimated the total addition to French and American gold balances from the end of 1929 to June 1931 at $1,084 million. Movements in such bulk were calculated to intensify prevailing fears. Moreover it will be clear that gold transferred on such a scale if not fully re-employed for credit creation represented a loss of purchasing power of impressive dimensions. This factor was so substantial as to lead many authorities to regard it as in itself a sufficient determinant of the world depression. It is suggested, however, that the facts are more in harmony with the contention that financial policy was responsible for the mal-distribution of gold rather than the converse.

The fall in prices was not due to restriction of credit enforced by the loss of gold. Rather the trader was faced with conditions which deprived him of sufficient profit-earning opportunities to enable him to make use even of the existing credit facilities.

Conflicting international financial policy, it will be observed, has exercised a four-fold influence tending to depress the price level. Deflationist countries have been compelled to pursue further deflation in order to bring the prices of their exportable goods into competitive relation with those of inflationist countries. Reparation and War debts have exerted the same effect in an intensified degree, consequent upon the necessity at all costs of creating an export surplus. The drain on the resources of debtor countries to carry out fixed-charge obligations in face of falling prices has gradually isolated certain areas as danger centres. These countries, debarred from the long-term credit market, have curtailed their purchases and made every effort to force sales. Since, however, the debts and obligations have remained, their discharge has involved a steady drain of gold in default of other means of payment. When it is remembered that the weakened economic structure was in any case hard beset by the effects of the world-wide stock-market collapse, it will be realized that the dangerous and continuous inconsistencies of international policy were bound to strain powers of resistance to the utmost.

The final touch to the stage-setting for a world financial crisis came from the attempted avoidance of the risks of long-term investment by the substitution of short-term bank loans. As already mentioned, this was the expedient by which Germany was maintaining her precarious balance. The growth of foreign short-term deposits was occasioning considerable anxiety in London also, as witness the attention paid to the subject in the Macmillan Report. It was becoming clear that an alarm in Europe might easily precipitate a financial *débâcle* in Germany; but the further question exercising the mind of the external observer was the degree of stability attaching to this country. Could we be counted upon as a bulwark against the storm or, far otherwise, was our impending collapse the supreme menace in the world situation? Many people at home viewed our position with misgiving. In addition to the Macmillan Committee, which surveyed the whole field of internal and international credit and reported in June 1931, the Sir George May Committee had been appointed to report specially upon the condition and prospects of the State's budget of revenue and expenditure. Nevertheless, while these steps indicated serious anxiety at home, few people recognized the extent of the deterioration of British credit in foreign estimation.

The causes of this apprehension require further consideration.

AS OTHERS SAW US

In troublous times the foreign depositor has regarded the banks of this country as a safe repository for his funds mainly for two reasons.

In the first place the soundness of British budgetary practice has given protection against a decline of Government credit. There are various stages of weakening credit. The first is inability to fulfil debt redemption; the second, borrowing for current expenditure; the last is borrowing by means of forced bank loans and inflation

MONETARY CHAOS AND THE FALL IN THE PRICE LEVEL

of the currency. In this last stage the depreciation of the currency is exacting toll upon all creditors. The end of the process everybody now knows is to render the currency unit worthless; consequently, bonds and obligations entitled to a fixed payment in the currency unit also become worthless and floating capital is wiped out.

In 1931, the foreign observer thought we had passed the first phase and were about to enter the second. In addition to the general trend he noted the heavy capital item of death duties[1] treated as income; and the mounting cost of unemployment.

The second special advantage attaching to a sterling deposit was the strength of our international financial position, giving protection against exchange depreciation. In the past, as has been mentioned, we could always turn the balance of payments in our favour at short notice by merely allowing a large amount of foreign acceptances to mature; or, taking a longer view, the only question to be decided was the sum-total of investment available for lending abroad. On balance, the year's trading was bound to show a surplus in our favour, for not only was ours the most flourishing export trade in the world, but shipping earnings, interest dues and financial commissions constituted a substantial addition to the national income from overseas.

[1] Estimated at £90 million in April 1931 budget. Revised to £83 million in Emergency Budget, but only £65 million reached.

But by 1931 it seemed that the foundations of this position had been sapped. Our relative share of the world's export trade had been declining since the end of the year, and the total of world trade since the slump had been undergoing severe contraction. This in itself involved a reduction in shipping earnings and bill-broking commissions, while overseas investment earnings were bound to suffer from the state of trade and, in some cases, from default of other countries.

Meanwhile, there was very little evidence of a curtailment of our purchases abroad, so that it became common knowledge that our powerfully established position of creditor nation had at length been lost, and that the year's trade would show us to be called upon for payments exceeding our dues.

This in itself was a serious blow to financial prestige, but the immediate threat to the exchange position was of a more pressing nature. We were no longer able to turn the foreign exchanges in our favour at short notice by allowing acceptances to run off. In recent years the importance of this factor was outweighed by the tremendous volume of short-term deposits on foreign account, which, in time of panic, might be withdrawn in such mass as to make it impossible to obtain foreign currency in sufficient amount to make full payment. Anxiety in this respect called in question the confidence previously displayed abroad in the protection provided by a sterling deposit against exchange depreciation.

MONETARY CHAOS AND THE FALL IN THE PRICE LEVEL

It will be clear that this country was between the upper and the nether millstone, the former at home, the latter abroad.

At home our anxieties were: reduced trade, growing unemployment and increased taxation. These threatened State solvency and credit.

Abroad, our troubles were: a higher internal price level relative to world prices, diminished export trade, reduced earnings on "invisible" exports, heavy liabilities on short term. In conjunction with the home situation the threat to the sterling exchange was certainly very real.

It was in this atmosphere of doubt and anxiety that the country had to meet the financial storm that broke over Europe in the middle of 1931.

FINANCIAL CATACLYSM—A BRIEF RECAPITULATION

It has been mentioned that the first storm-cloud to appear on the horizon was the announcement by the Austrian Government in the latter part of May of the impending insolvency of an important bank, the Credit Anstalt. The Bank of England came to the rescue, but this could not prevent the exposure of weakness in Central Europe, making creditors of Germany anxious to repatriate their funds. Immediately large withdrawals of funds put great pressure on the mark exchange.

President Hoover made a bid to restore confidence with a proposal on June 20th of a one year's moratorium for all War-debt payments. The first good effects of this proposal, however, were dissipated by delay. For France the proposals meant a reduction of budgetary income at a period when receipts generally were falling.

French acceptance with modifications was not announced until the first week in July, by which time the pressure on the German banks had recommenced. In the interval, a loan of $100 million had been granted to the Reichsbank jointly by the Bank of International Settlements, the Federal Reserve Bank of New York, the Bank of England and the Bank of France. This proved quite insufficient to stem the tide of withdrawals, which before the middle of July had risen to M.100 million a day. On July 13th the Darmstadter und Nationalbank suspended payment. The German Government ordered all banks and the Stock Exchange to close for two days. A decree was issued exempting banks and private persons from meeting their obligations to make payment until further notice. After the expiration of the two days, on July 16th the banks were opened with orders to make only essential payments. The Government having failed to raise fresh credits abroad, the Reichsbank resorted to the weapon of the discount rate which had been wielded with vigour and effect in previous crises. The discount rate was raised to 10 per cent and the Lombard rate (rate for loans against collateral) to 15 per cent. It was obvious that the Central Banks' loan originally granted for three weeks was a "frozen credit." To what extent were other banks involved? How would they stand the strain? Fear spread towards Great Britain. Heavy withdrawals of foreign balances caused an unprecedented outflow of gold. In nine days the efflux from the Bank of England amounted to over £25,000,000. The Bank Rate, which had been raised from 2½ to 3½ per cent on July 23rd, was raised to 4½ per cent on July 30th. The Bank of England was meantime completing arrangements by which the Bank of France and the Federal Reserve Bank of New York each placed £25,000,000 to its credit in their respective currencies. On the last day of July, however, Sir George May's Committee had reported to the public on the state of the national exchequer, estimating a probable budget deficiency of £120,000,000 for the ensuing year. The foreign view was that the report confirmed their worst fears and that British credit was at breaking-point. This was certainly the case in Germany. But the Reichsbank unfalteringly applied its weapon. The discount rate was raised to 15 per cent on August 1st, the Lombard rate of 20 per cent. The most rigorous control of all foreign exchange dealings was also instituted. These measures achieved remarkable success. In the early part of August, the banks announced that they were prepared to satisfy all demands in full. The Reichsbank was able a little later to show an improvement in its gold holdings and devisen (foreign exchange holdings). The storm centre was shifting to Great Britain, where a political crisis of the first order was caused by the financial crisis. The May Committee had made it an essential part of their recommendations that a main constituent of retrenchment should be a saving on the unemployment benefit allowances. The attitude of the Government to this recommendation was regarded abroad as the test question. Disagreement in the Cabinet provoked fresh withdrawals from the Bank. On August 24th the Labour Government resigned, and the next day the National Government was formed. Thereafter a new attempt was made to strengthen the sterling exchange. A credit of £80,000,000 was arranged jointly with France and America, this time directly with the Treasuries of the countries concerned.

A few days later, Mr. Snowden introduced a Supplementary Budget in the House of Commons covering an estimated deficiency of £74,680,000 for the current year. The deficiency for 1932–33 was estimated at £170 million on the previously existing basis of revenue and taxation. The new proposals would convert the deficit into a surplus in each case, with provision for redemption of debt amounting to £46·3 million for 1931–32 and £52 million for 1932–33.

The immediate effect of the budget proposals and their apparent acceptance without demur by the public was to create a favourable impression abroad. This good impression was immediately effaced and profound misgiving substituted in its place by news of a manifestation of British sailors against reduced pay. If there was one thing which had acquired a legendary significance in countries abroad as a symbol of rock-like stability more marked than that of the Bank of England, it was the British Navy. It seemed to the foreigner that all his long-cherished beliefs were being challenged. The further shock was too much. On September 16th the Bank lost in gold £5,000,000, on the 17th, £10,000,000, on the 18th, £18,000,000. Further credits were refused. It was obvious the *dénouement* was near. On Saturday morning the Stock Exchange was due to open for the first time on a Saturday since 1917. Government securities, especially in New York, were freely offered and difficult to sell. In the latter centre, sterling was at one time offered below the gold point and England was virtually off the gold standard. In two months, the Bank of England had lost in gold and foreign exchange a sum of more than £200,000,000. Instead of fighting the battle with a repressive discount rate, the authorities wisely decided to accept the verdict of the facts. On Monday, the 21st, the following announcement was made:

His Majesty's Government have decided, after consultation with the Bank of England, that it has become necessary to suspend for the time being the operation of Sub-section 2, Section 1 of the Gold Standard Act of 1925, which requires the Bank to sell gold at a fixed price. A Bill for this purpose will be introduced immediately and it is the intention of His Majesty's Government to pass it through all its stages Monday, September 21st. In the meantime, the Bank of England has been authorized to proceed accordingly in anticipation of the action of Parliament.

The Stock Exchange was closed for two days, and, suceeding this announcement, almost all foreign Bourses, except Paris, closed also. On the same Monday, sterling was offered down to below $4, but later recovered to $4·22½.

A new chapter in Britain's and the world's financial history had opened.

CHAPTER III

A BLESSING IN DISGUISE

The culmination of the series of momentous events related in the preceding section has been variously interpreted in its auguries for the future. In some quarters the view has been expressed that the outcome should be beneficial to the interests of trade, but inimical to those of finance. The distinction appears to be without justification on a broad view. Financial prosperity obviously cannot be maintained on a basis of declining trade. Wisely handled the present situation affords not only the prospect of improved trade conditions, but a recovery of financial hegemony among the nations of the world such as would have seemed impossible a year ago.

CREDIT

An investigation of this aspect of the subject invites a retrospective glance at the apprehensions and predictions of foreign and home observers current at the close of last year to which reference has been made.

It will be generally agreed at the outset that these apprehensions were founded on a correct diagnosis of the trend of affairs. The respect engendered by the foresight and perspicacity of many such observers is somewhat dimmed however by more recent happenings. In so far as the flight from the pound was originally determined by the *trend* of events it was in line with the facts. In such matters intangible influences count for much. Credit after all is only confidence, so that the psychological elements and estimation of the future are at the root of the matter. But it is possible for a trend to be arrested. Such being the case it calls attention to the undoubted fact that the *actualities* as apart from the *trend* never warranted a flight from sterling, whether the factor chiefly feared was the consequences of an unbalanced budget or the adverse balance of trade. In so far as the former factor predominated the transferors are faced with a paradox. Their funds have been removed from a country which has not only balanced its budget, but has interpreted its obligations in a sterner sense than is freely applied abroad. That is, it has regarded the statutory provisions for redemption of debt as a charge upon revenue. The funds transferred, however, were in large measure deposited in countries where a balanced budget still remained an aspiration.

In France the French Senate has recently passed into law the budget provisions for the nine months to December 31, 1932. (For nine months only owing to a new arrangement by which the financial year coincides with the calendar year.) The estimates purport to show a surplus, but this surplus will almost certainly prove illusory. The Rapporteur Général to the Senate places the deficiency at frs. 3,000 million on the existing basis of expenditure which, however, he regards as certain to be exceeded. Moreover, in the preceding two years deficits have not been fully provided for in subsequent budgets, the Treasury Reserves having been drawn upon to the extent of some frs. 5,000 million. The growing deficits on the French State Railway system are another embarrassment, as is also the tendency of many of the larger companies to seek State guarantees for their loans. Thus the Compagnie Transatlantique has received guarantees for loans exceeding frs. 460 million. Further sums have gone towards reorganizing various banks.

In America, too, difficulty has been experienced in balancing the budget, although their scale of taxation is much lower than we are accustomed to in this country. For the financial year ending June 1932 the deficit will be the greatest in peace-time history. After a struggle it seems that adequate new taxation has been imposed to obviate the deficiency which would have ensued for the year 1932–33 on the basis of previously existing revenue and expenditure.

The budget deficiency for the current year has been met by State borrowing. In view of the amount of the deficiency this method of dealing with the situation has provoked criticism. Possibly the critics have in mind the recent amendment to the Federal Reserve Act by which Government securities rank as part backing for the Federal Reserve note issue.

It is not surprising that French financial opinion has viewed such procedure with undisguised concern, largely determining, in fact, the withdrawal of French balances in America. At times these withdrawals for French account and those of other countries have been carried out on a scale which has even threatened the maintenance of the gold standard in America. This was especially the case in October last when in one week no less than $153·8 million was earmarked for foreign account (that is, set aside for export) in addition to $28 million actually engaged for export, two-thirds of which went to France. This desire to withdraw has been further manifested whenever proposals have been mooted for stimulating trade by credit expansion schemes.

Looking back it is abundantly clear that the policy of transferring deposits from this country, on the ground of the instability of the British budget or of its comparative inferiority *vis-à-vis* foreign budgets, received no support from the facts. It may be, however, that the chief reason for withdrawal of deposits was related to the growing deterioration of our trade balance and consequent fears of exchange depreciation. In so far as the withdrawals occurred before September 21st last they were justified by the event. It is quite certain, however, that the burden upon the sterling exchange involved by the adverse balance for 1931 on income account only would not in itself have occasioned the abrogation of the gold standard. The change was necessitated by move-

A BLESSING IN DISGUISE

ments on capital account which set up an outward flow of far greater magnitude than the adverse balance on current items. It was mentioned by the Chancellor of the Exchequer that withdrawals in the two months preceding the abandonment of the gold standard exceeded £200 million. This sum much exceeded the entire deficiency on the balance of payments for the whole of the year 1931. The extent of this deficiency is still to some degree a matter of estimate, but it may be fairly assumed that the figure compiled by the *Board of Trade Journal* (reproduced in the Appendix) is a reasonably close approximation to the facts. This computation assesses the adverse balance for 1931 at £110 million, comparing with a favourable balance of £28 million for 1930 and £103 million for 1929. The bulk of the adverse balance for last year was attributable to the general decline in world trade. Thus the reduced income from shipping, overseas investment and financial commissions was of the order of £170 million. The portion due to excess of merchandise imports over exports exceeded that for 1930 by only £30 million.

The adverse balance so disclosed, namely, £110 million, is subject to important reductions before the actual outflow of sterling apart from capital withdrawals is established. In 1931 there was a net export of gold amounting to £35 million. In addition to this there must have been an inflow of sterling on capital account due to repayments of loans by sinking fund operations and maturity redemptions. No estimates are available for the amount of this last factor in 1931, but in 1928 it was estimated by the *Economist* at £30 million and in 1929 by Sir Robert Kindersley at £48½ million. If the equivalent figure for 1931 is placed at £20 million it should prove to be an under-estimate. This would reduce the net adverse balance to half the original figure, making £55 million. It is clear that such a sum *per se* could not account for the course of events in the latter part of last year. Comparatively it amounts to little more than for an individual who has been a good customer over a number of years to the local tradesmen drawing a little on his credit in a time of difficulty. As a matter of comparison it may be noted that on a balance of payments for 1930 showing a favourable margin of £23 million,[1] our overseas investments amounted to £109 million.

The real reason for our enforced departure from gold was therefore loss of credit, which on this head was due, as in the case of the budget factor, to the trend of affairs rather than existing actualities.

Sentiment abroad being governed by the belief that rapid economic deterioration had set in, it was inevitable that on the Continent the bitter experience of the past should not only make apprehension more keen, but recall previous parallels that had been painfully impressed on the memory of many. But even in America there was the same general despondency as to British prospects. The *Financial and Commercial Chronicle*, whose acumen

---

[1] Allowing for £5 million gold imports.

A BLESSING IN DISGUISE

in another connection was earlier commended, provides a good example in its comment upon the method agreed to in America for supplying a half-share of the first foreign credit arranged for the support of sterling. Cricicism was directed towards the arrangement by which the American share, which, it will be remembered, was for £25 million, was accorded by the New York Federal Reserve Bank (that is, the chief Central Bank) instead of by member banks or finance houses. The ground of the criticism, acute enough in itself, was evidently based on the belief that the accommodation granted would speedily prove itself to be a mere addition to the large blocks of "frozen credit" already immobilized in Europe. "Imagine the Bank of England being in a position to repay £50 million" in external currency in a few months, was the comment made, suggesting that the formal expression of the notion carried its own refutation.

The opinion definitely predominant abroad that sterling would sink to a mere fraction of its former gold or commodity value received widespread credence in this country also. The public were invited to protect themselves against the devastating effects of inflation by exchanging all fixed charges (i.e. carrying an obligation to payment of a specific sum in sterling, which would therefore depreciate in value with the currency) for assets that would advance in monetary value with the rise in the price level, such as houses, commodities and equity or ordinary shares. The time at which a danger of this character was a distinct possibility was that immediately succeeding the abandonment of gold. Had the general public become highly alarmed and communicated panic to the foreign depositor a very grave situation would have arisen, probably necessitating closure of the banks and re-opening under controlled conditions. The danger was heightened by the readiness of unscrupulous exchange-wreckers to seek their own profit in provoking calamity. In such circumstances it is quite easy to picture a collapse of sterling and the European financial structure as the price of failure to impart early confidence. As it was, however, the generality of British investors and depositors were quite unperturbed by what occurred, and regarded the heavy marking down in the prices of Government stocks—which was caused by liquidation accompanying the calling in of foreign deposits—as a good opportunity to acquire sound investments at attractive levels. Happily they proved to be right, the recovery in gilt-edged quotations from the low levels of 1931 being very satisfactory.

When the risks and fears of the autumn are remembered it enables the nature and value of the subsequent complete transformation to be more fully appreciated. Most of the predictions freely made at the time have been falsified. The budget has been balanced, note circulation is somewhat diminished, the cost of living is slightly lower, Clearing Bank deposits are (unfortunately) reduced, foreign supporting loans have been largely repaid.

It is a statement of plain fact that British credit has

been wonderfully re-established. The faith of foreign investors in the sterling deposit has been restored. It has even been necessary to establish the Exchange Equalization Fund partly to prevent foreign speculators raising the sterling exchange by their purchases to an unwelcome level.

In the meantime we may be well satisfied that events, though shaped to some extent by misconception and exaggeration, took the course that made financial history. Had it been otherwise it might have been possible to carry on for some time much as before: a patched-up budget and serious misgivings on the balance of trade would have led perhaps to a special committee of enquiry or a publicity campaign. Eventually the public concern might have been allayed by the introduction of Protection, which would have proved a very poor substitute for cutting loose from the gold parity incubus.

TRADE PROS AND CONS

The trading community hailed the relinquishment of the gold standard with expressions of relief—almost of jubilation. Of the immediate benefit no doubt could exist. The reason is clear enough; British goods are bought with sterling and sterling was cheapened in foreign currency.

Now that the early excitement has died down, it is

possible to review calmly the gains and losses resulting from the step taken.

One gain is outstanding. It has already been stated that at the time of our return to the gold standard in 1925 the internal level of prices was above that of the leading markets in the world and therefore imposed a severe handicap on traders. The hope that the world price level would rise to meet our own was not realized; there is, moreover, ground for believing that the handicap was increased rather than removed, and would progressively have encroached on our ability to maintain our relative position in a condition of world trade where competition is heightened by the scarcity of orders. The exporter selling goods in foreign currency was in effect asking too much for his wares. The burden of disadvantage was an exceedingly serious one: estimates place it at more than 20 per cent at the time of our departure from the gold standard. Assuming that we have learnt the lesson of past experience we should not again make the mistake of harnessing trade to an exchange stabilized at above its true world level. Meantime the Exchange Equalization Fund of £150 million should suffice to protect the trader against a violent rebound of foreign sentiment which would carry the exchange to an unduly high level. The trading community is therefore reasonably assured of the removal of their previous handicap. This in itself constitutes a relief of the first importance. But it is not all.

A BLESSING IN DISGUISE

There can be little question that the departure from gold has been a material factor in facilitating the decline in rates of interest which the world is now experiencing, and to which, as a succeeding chapter will show, great importance attaches. In particular, the financial policy of this country is no longer ordered by the necessity to conserve a scanty stock of metal.

It could hardly be expected that benefits of so sweeping a nature would be gained without any offsetting disadvantages. As far as we at home are concerned these have not been material. It has been said that the increase in the cost of living which many anticipated has not occurred; consequently our production costs have not increased to any extent, nor do we suffer any real hardship from the reduced gold value of the interest payments due to us on capital invested in foreign countries. Indeed, the fact that overseas countries can buy the sterling they need to discharge their obligations at a cheaper rate is really remedial having regard to the fact that the exaggeration of debt burdens by the fall in prices is one of the greatest of current problems.

It is not in these respects that the net gains of our abandonment of gold suffer any substantial diminution. It is rather in the embarrassment caused by the tremendous readjustment of prices which has been necessitated in the gold-standard countries, the occurrence of which has prevented our feeling the effects of a depreciated exchange through the medium of an increase in home prices. In order to retain their hold on foreign markets the countries "on gold" have been compelled to adjust their prices to a level which enables them to compete with the possible alternative source of supply provided by the countries "off gold." The further fall added to the previous decline was particularly hurtful. The burden of fixed obligations in the countries affected has thereby been increased, and the volume of world trade has suffered further contraction by loss of profit margin and buying incentive.

THE STERLING EXCHANGE

When this situation is duly appreciated it will be recognized that a financial policy designed to exaggerate the exchange discount and create an export bounty is not a sound one. It savours too much of the unending sequence of attempts "to outflank the other fellow" which has already caused so much economic disaster. In the long run instead of all manœuvring for position it is better to start "all square." By manipulating the exchange to an artificially low level, while having at the same time imposed tariffs against foreign imports, this country would be guilty of reintroducing exactly those disturbing influences in world trade (excluding imports while forcing exports) which have already proved so harmful and which our publicists have so consistently deplored in others. This would be a poor lead from a country which is universally regarded as a guide in

A BLESSING IN DISGUISE

matters of international trade and finance. It would, moreover, be the essence of unwisdom for a country more dependent than any other on world trade.

The actual exchange level to be aimed at is more easily decided in principle than in practice.

The underlying factors which determine the "theoretical" parity of currencies above and below which the actual quotations oscillate have already been briefly referred to. The clue to the principle relating the foreign exchanges is that quotations tend to be drawn towards that level at which goods of like nature are expressed at like value, expense of removal and obstacles to transfer being eliminated. More accurately, the ultimate relationship of the currencies of different countries is to be found in terms of their respective internal purchasing powers. The "theoretical" equilibrium is itself constantly changing and the actual quotations only by accident ever exactly harmonize with the "theoretical" values. A number of factors may be responsible for the variation. Perhaps the most important is that of market anticipations of the future trend; another, as we in this country know to our cost, is a rigid internal structure by which interior maladjustment may be sustained for years.

The view taken by English economists is that the true purchasing power parity lies somewhere between $3·40 and rather under $4. As a matter of fact, the complications are such that it does not seem possible to establish the equilibrium level within narrow limits.

It is, of course, to be hoped that the purchasing power of gold will tend to fall—in other words, that world prices will rise. This is, indeed, the essential condition of a return of world prosperity. If world prices do rise it will be desirable to allow sterling prices to keep step with the upward movement. By so doing the exchange rate would be unaffected.

The question at the moment, however, is this, Can this country by financial policy stimulate the flow of international trade and a rise in world prices?

It seems probable that a somewhat bolder approach to this question is justified by comparison with that which seemed necessary immediately after our departure from gold. At that time there was no expectation of an early return of foreign confidence. All efforts were directed towards stemming the decline in the exchange level. It is true, however, that the balance of payments on income account is still adverse and likely to remain so for some time. Necessarily this limits our powers of initiative, but not to the extent that is sometimes imagined.

The balance of payments is the subject of a good deal of misconception. It is generally treated as though it were a rigid structure to which something can be added or taken away according to need, but that if subjected to irregular stresses, it collapses. In fact, however, the balance of payments is not rigid in nature at all but essentially plastic. In the past few years it has been subject to every manner of buffeting and violence and yet has shown the most astonishing resilience. The more apt metaphor would be that of a child's balloon, but made of a very tough material. Squeeze it, and it bulges somewhere else; pull it, and some part contracts. It is not until the fabric has been weakened by almost intolerable ill-treatment that the risk of breakage—or literally exchange collapse—causes anxiety. The plasticity is far more pronounced in the case of a country off gold where a balance is preserved by the movement of exchange rates. Some people have feared that we were in danger of persistently buying in excess of capacity to make payment, overlooking the effect such a procedure would exercise in depreciating the exchange, thus making foreign goods dearer and our own cheaper.

The price of this plasticity, however, is a fluctuating exchange which is a handicap to trade relationships by adding a further and substantial risk to overseas business. The establishment of the Exchange Equalization Fund has for its object the mitigation of this short-term fluctuation and the orderly control of the general trend.

The existence of an adverse balance on income account must, nevertheless, limit our potentialities and influence in overseas affairs. But even in the crisis of last autumn it has been shown that the departure from gold was caused by movements on capital account rather than by an adverse income account. And this despite the fact that in this country a marked disequilibrium had been maintained for years.

At the present time it would seem likely that movements on capital account favour this country and tend to offset a continued but diminished adverse balance on income account.

What is happening at the moment is that overseas interest earnings, financial commissions and shipping dues are continuing to decline with the contraction of world trade. From our point of view this means less purchasing power to continue to take goods previously imported from overseas countries. The result is further to diminish the latter's trade, which sets up a vicious circle. It would be desirable to maintain normal purchases from most countries, especially those which in the past have previously looked to this country for development loans, largely, of course, the Dominions and Crown Colonies. This is the minimum required in order to avoid further weakening of the position of the new countries. As it is likely that food and raw material purchases will continue to maintain an almost surprising buoyancy it seems probable this end will be achieved. The loss of interest and financial earnings affecting the investing section of the community will not substantially reduce consumption capacity while the exchange remains firm. Such loss of interest as occurs will reflect a lapse of return on past savings and can only be compensated by new or hoarded savings finding an outlet in investment. Despite reduced profits and earnings there is at present no lack of ability to find funds for suitable investment since large sums of money are lying industrially idle on short-term deposits. The problem is to find credit-worthy borrowers; that is, enterprises, or public bodies, able to employ loans remuneratively. In some directions, however, opportunities will present themselves. Every advantage should be taken to utilize them to the full, more especially such as would set up direct and indirect demands for British exports; direct demands by actual placing of contracts, and, indirect, by providing the flow of exchange which would make imports from this country possible. Given these conditions the strain upon the sterling exchange would be limited. It will doubtless be found capable of sustaining reasonable demands of this character. The emergence of some degree of regional prosperity would probably be a first step toward influencing a broader recovery. It may well be that it will first occur in all that group of countries which has allied itself to the sterling exchange. It has been said that in certain cases trade may be stimulated by granting further loan accommodation. In this connection it is important to remember that only six countries now remain effectively on the gold standard: Belgium, France, Holland, South Africa, Switzerland, and the United States. Germany and some of the small European countries must be placed in a category by themselves. Most of the other nations have substantially followed the financial fortunes of this country.

A remarkable opportunity has thus been afforded us for the recovery of much of the financial prestige and initiative which the events of recent years have impaired. On the whole this is a well-deserved reward for our leaders in the banking sphere, whose ability, strenuous efforts, and public spirit—in the international sense—have hitherto received but scant recognition.

Our ultimate prospects of regaining ascendancy in this field, when our powers are more fully restored, seem bright, as both France and America appear disinclined to take the initiative. In France severe losses have resulted from loans to a group of countries mainly in close political union with herself. These losses following upon those sustained in Russia since the War, and coinciding with a great movement for the repatriation of foreign funds, would suggest that France is unlikely to enter willingly into the field of international finance on a large scale.

In America a Commission appointed by the Senate recently took evidence in regard to the machinery and methods adopted for placing many of the foreign loans made by America between 1925-28, most of which proved disastrous investments, some for intrinsic reasons, but mainly as the result of external events. The ultimate conclusion of the Commission was the desirability of restricting activities in the field of overseas lending.

A BLESSING IN DISGUISE

MONETARY POLICY AND THE HOME PRICE LEVEL

The assumption on which much of the above argument is based is that the sterling exchange will prove its underlying strength. After the abandonment of gold the chief concern of the monetary authorities was to prevent a rise in home prices. It was feared that depreciation of the exchange would lead to an increase in the cost of living due to the higher cost of imports. Higher prices at home would cause a demand for further credit which, in turn, would raise prices and cause a further depreciation of the exchange, and so on, in the well-known dangerous sequence.

The fear of serious exchange depreciation, however, has now subsided, and the anxiety to prevent a rise in the home prices has been succeeded by a widespread demand that monetary policy shall be framed with the deliberate object of promoting a rise in the price level. Many who regard a policy of this nature with favour find it necessary to be careful of their friends, some of whom appear to minimize the difficulties and dangers associated with such a course of action.

It is true that the powers of the Bank of England are not limited to the influence which it exercises upon the terms of credit by variations in the bank-rate. It has, further, the capacity to enlarge or reduce the credit base upon which the broader credit superstructure of the Joint-Stock Banks is built. This latter purpose is achieved by means of what are known as "open-market operations." The Bank of England, by purchasing Government Securities (or Bills of Exchange, or by granting loans) in the market enlarges the credit base owing to the fact that the ultimate result is normally to put one of the Joint-Stock Banks in credit with the Bank of England by the sum received in exchange for the Securities. But a balance at the Bank of England is regarded by the former as the equivalent of cash and therefore its capacity for lending or investment is increased if a constant ratio of reserves to liabilities is to be maintained.

Business conditions during a deflationary movement, however, will be such that the legitimate trade demand for increased accommodation is dormant and therefore the banking system is confronted with the difficulty of putting the created purchasing power into industrial circulation. The possibility has to be considered of stimulating the direct demand by special expedients such as the placing of orders by public bodies. But here again the Exchequer situation opposes obstacles which at present seem insurmountable. Apart from this there is the danger that even if the forcing tactics adopted produce a response in the price level, the rise may prove merely a spasmodic spurt, so that the subsequent fall will leave matters worse than they were before. On the other hand, if the upward movement is sustained by measures that undermine confidence the rise will be converted into an inflationary movement that may

A BLESSING IN DISGUISE

develop beyond control. It is not suggested that these objections exclude every scheme for stimulating the trade demand for credit.[1] To many, however, it seems improbable that in our present position any sound scheme of credit expansion can be devised by means of which an *immediate* response in the price level can be secured. There remain, however, the indirect and more gradual results which are to be derived from open-market operations in reducing the long-term rate of interest and providing a cheap and abundant supply of credit to industry.

The first effect of the purchase of Government Securities by the Bank of England is naturally to raise the price of investment stocks. The upward movement will be carried further by the subsequent action of the Joint-Stock Banks if these, unable to obtain remunerative employment for their additional resources in trade, are impelled to increase their investments in gilt-edged securities. The diminished return on first-class securities will of course be reflected in the cheaper cost of borrowing to industry. This aspect of the subject will be further analysed in Chapter V, where it will be argued that the long-term rate of interest is not only a potent but ultimately a determining factor in influencing the course of prices and trade.

A perusal of the ensuing chapter should meanwhile

[1] Later some attention will be given to the expedients adopted in America with a view to this end.

demonstrate clearly that the international financial situation is such that the money markets of the world are subject to constant underlying anxiety and sudden scares. Therefore a policy of the nature indicated would be materially assisted by, and may actually require, the collaboration of the chief financial centres of the world. If it were generally known that the central banks of the world were unitedly grappling with the situation a measure of confidence would be imparted to the public mind, thus supplying an essential element in revival which is now lacking.

ULTIMATE RETURN TO GOLD

Looking back on recent events it already seems safe to say that the policy of relinquishing the gold standard as an alternative to a repressive deflationary policy, with its crushing money rates and social disturbance, has been vindicated. Indeed, it would appear that had the decision to be taken again in similar circumstances and in the light of subsequent events no other choice would be made on the main issue. Not only so, but the improvement achieved seems so impressive that no thought can be entertained of a hasty or premature return to a gold basis.

Future policy in this respect depends on a balancing of the relative advantages and disadvantages.

The advantage of a stable exchange rate to trade cannot be questioned; but it would be dearly bought at the price of renewed instablity of the general price level arising from conflicting national policies, and exaggerated by mass movements of metal. Thus the undoubted benefit of day to day steadiness has to be weighed against the even more important factor of sustained stability. As matters stand at present a mere return to the gold standard without co-operation or agreed policy would seem a rash proceeding—even assuming a satisfactory outcome to future discussions on War debts and reparations.

It may therefore be reasonably assumed that negotiations of an international character will be opened on the question of a general restoration of the gold standard and the main principles of future central bank co-operation.

Among the many issues to be subsequently decided will be that of the basis of stabilization for sterling. It is vital that the level chosen should not be one which involves a repetition of the long-drawn-out miseries of deflation. Even an honourable desire to repay our creditors on the terms of the original contract could not justify the choice of an artificially high level; nor would it be justified by the fact that the value of interest receipts on capital previously invested abroad would thereby be enhanced. An overvalued currency with its disastrous reactions on trade cannot be entertained. The level selected must be that which appears to express the natural purchasing power of sterling in relation to those of the predominant gold standard countries.

CHAPTER IV

REPERCUSSIONS ABROAD AND THE EXTERNAL SITUATION GENERALLY

EXTERNAL REPERCUSSIONS

Externally the effects of the momentous change in British currency policy were varied. To those countries remaining on gold it has unfortunately proved in its early repercussions the reverse of helpful. For some others following in the wake of sterling the relief has been immediate. In cheapening sterling relatively to the gold value of a proportion of their exports, it has provided just that easement of the burden of overseas debt which the debtor countries, such as Australia and the Argentine, required. It is probable that the additional premium on such of her goods as she sells to gold countries will provide Australia with that few extra millions she needs to balance her overseas payments, the reason, of course, being that gold values have not fallen in the same proportion as sterling, which is the currency in which the bulk of Australia's overseas debts were contracted.

INDIA

As far as India is concerned the change has amounted almost to financial salvation. The anxiety and difficulty

THE EXTERNAL SITUATION

of the first three quarters of the year 1931 for those responsible for maintaining the credit of India may not be generally recognized, but was, nevertheless, a financial factor of the first order. It is incumbent on critics who would have had us maintain the gold standard by means of a high discount rate to show how the special difficulty of India could then have been met. The anxiety was not primarily the budget position, though for India, in common with all other countries throughout the world, that problem was not an easy one. The chief trial and task was the collection of sterling to meet home obligations. Normally the Indian Treasury through its Ways and Means Department collects sterling by the simple process of purchasing the claims of native exporters on overseas buyers. The Indian producer, however, was suffering, again in common with those of all countries, from the low price of commodities, and this in turn led to a demand on the part of this section of the community for a lower rupee value. Despite repeated assurances that no change in the value of the rupee entered into the Government's considerations, anticipation was growing that the rate would be reduced to 1s. 4d. in place of 1s. 6d. Having regard also to the nervousness engendered by the political disturbances it is not surprising that capital was being expatriated. So far therefore from Ways and Means being able to purchase sterling, they were constantly forced to supply sterling by drafts based on the gold backing of the currency, causing severe depletion of this part of the reserve. In view of its inability to acquire sterling by the usual process the Government of India in May 1931 raised a loan in the London market carrying 6 per cent interest, this operation following by a few months an earlier issue bearing 5½ per cent. It was known that in the following January a previous loan to the amount of £15 million matured, and was likely to require, as it seemed, another loan for the purpose. In face of these conditions it was not surprising that the May issue met with but a small public response, so that the underwriters were called upon to take up the major portion, and the scrip was quoted at a discount on the Stock Exchange. The political situation, the failure of the issue and its discount in the market, caused extreme weakness in Indian stocks. In the July following the Prime Minister made a statement in the House of Commons to the effect that the British Government would render financial assistance to India, if the need arose, to maintain her credit. It was at this stage that the Austro–German credit storm burst upon Europe, and, speedily travelling towards London, threatened British credit and its power to fulfil the promise made. By this time the available gold for further sterling drafts had dwindled to the scantiest amount, and, together with the situation in the capital market, raised the spectre of sheer inability on the part of either Government to carry out its obligations.

Before the impending menace had been generally

THE EXTERNAL SITUATION

recognized, however, Great Britain took her historic step, and this was immediately followed by an ordinance of the Governor-General of India relieving the Government there of the necessity to sell sterling or gold. Considerable uncertainty ruled upon this announcement, and the banks were closed for three days; but a further proclamation which soon followed stating that the rupee would be linked with sterling exchange immediately cleared the atmosphere. It was greeted with the same confidence as that shown in this country after the September 21st decision. Sterling was again made available; but within a fortnight applications had ceased and the exchange had recovered to parity. Then came into operation a new factor unheralded and totally unexpected, like many another, which has subsequently marked a turning-point in history. The Indian cultivator, hit by the fall in commodity prices, and with fixed payments for rent and interest additionally burdensome as elsewhere, was tempted by the substantial profit offered him to sell his gold. The movement spread and a regular stream of gold exports continued to flow, a stream which like the quality of mercy was twice blessed, for it not only restored Indian credit but provided a powerful support to the sterling exchange at a critical period, being an important factor in enabling the British Government to acquire the dollars and francs needed to meet first foreign withdrawals, and later the sums required in order to repay the special French and American credits raised for the support of sterling. The

Indian Government was able to meet the January maturity of £15 million without fresh borrowing. The ability to make the repayment was followed by a substantial improvement in Indian credit, reflected in the market quotations for the various issues. Not only so, but trade benefited. The gold released was so much buried purchasing power brought into effective use to the benefit of Indian trades and the British exporter.

FRANCE

It has been mentioned that a large part of the Indian gold stream flowed into France, but the stream was a mere trickle compared with that reaching her from America. During the autumn of 1931 French withdrawals from America in two months reached the heavy total of nearly $350 million. The drain was resumed in the new year, especially when measures regarded as of an inflationary nature were under discussion in America. The appetite of the French for gold has so far appeared insatiable, the stock at the Bank of France at May 27, 1932, being frs. 79·4 milliards.[1] The increase in 1931 in itself was greater than the present stock of the Bank of England. Nothing seems more certain than that French withdrawals in bulk are about to cease, and may be succeeded by a reverse movement since France herself is likely to enter upon a new economic phase.

[1] Over £600 million at par of exchange.

THE EXTERNAL SITUATION

Of late years a number of factors have combined to give the French a very powerful influence in world finance. Circumstances have combined to enable her to build up large claims in foreign monetary centres. The export surplus built up on a depreciated exchange, reparation payments, and the large earnings on tourist traffic, were at first mainly left abroad, subject to call at short notice. Foreign claims were fortified by a flight from the franc in the inflation period, and by the acquisition of large blocks of gold-standard exchange in the reconstruction period. The bulk of these foreign deposits were lodged in London and New York, which centres of course felt the strain when suddenly the European scare was started, and everywhere the nations were scurrying to withdraw and consolidate after the manner of a financial *sauve qui peut*. There are grounds for thinking that in future years France may not be unwilling to see some of her gold stock diminishing. The considerable French export surplus of preceding years was at least very severely impaired in 1931 when France first began to be seriously affected by the slump, but the influence of a reduced trade surplus was obscured by the repatriation of French funds, by which in effect she sold her foreign earning assets for gold—an unproductive asset if hoarded and one which in time of rising prices would lose in capital value also. Time will show whether this policy was wise. France was not seriously affected by the trade depression until much later than other countries. The failure of a financial syndicate known as the Oustric group in November 1930 dealt a serious blow to public confidence, and was followed in 1931 by the serious financial embarrassment of banks and building societies. Internal conditions were thus unstable before the financial crash in the middle of the year. The losses of the Bank of France on its sterling assets, amounting to nearly frs. 2,500 million and necessitating State support, were not calculated to allay uneasiness. The State was also called upon to guarantee the deposits of the Banque Nationale de Crédit and the Banque de l'Union Parisienne. Public apprehension revealed itself in an outbreak of hoarding. Stock Exchange prices of shares and bonds fell considerably, reflecting a decline in the volume of internal trade. Foreign trade at the beginning of 1932 was on almost exactly half the scale of two years previously. In 1931 the excess of merchandise imports was frs. 11,778 million, compared with frs. 9,514 million, although the total trade was 23 per cent less. Gross receipts from tourist traffic, which in 1929 totalled approximately £80 million, fell in 1931 to £12 million. Reparations payments have now ceased and seem unlikely to attain at any rate substantial dimensions in the future. If, as seems probable, the country is for a period to be burdened with the handicap of an overvalued exchange, it requires little imagination to envisage the entire disappearance of the French surplus on the international balance. This forecast of

THE EXTERNAL SITUATION

the trend of the French economic outlook is based purely on what are believed to be the outstanding economic factors of the situation, and as such is not influenced by sentimental considerations, much less ill will or any desire to depreciate French credit or prospects. The reactions of French policy to developments of this nature, should they occur, remain to be seen. So far the dominating characteristic of French policy has been protection of the internal market, and this policy has been intensified rather than relaxed as a consequence of recent developments. It is, indeed, difficult to imagine any substantial reversal of the protectionist principle in France owing to the economic structure of the country. This is founded on the maintenance of peasant agriculture, which in face of modern power-farming can only be achieved by the imposition of wheat duties of a phenomenal height. It has been calculated that it requires fifty French families on the land to feed themselves and fifty others, while in America twenty families on farms feed themselves and eighty others. The possibility of this system being abandoned seems extremely remote. Nor is it easy to imagine the industrialist being content to see the agriculturist protected and not himself. This means that the French price level, now that it is firmly attached to a gold basis, may prove when put to the test to be as rigid as our own which was previously considered a notable example of rigidity. The French export industries will therefore find it particularly hard to adjust themselves to the existing level of prices, especially as the internal level has recently shown signs of an upward movement. The need of the trading community to secure an advance in the world price level is reinforced as in our own case by financial considerations. Considerable sums of capital lent abroad by France in past years are either already unproductive or in danger of becoming so owing to the defaults of borrowers, who have been unable to pay interest by reason of the effect on their trade of the calamitous fall in commodity prices. An investigation into the destination of French foreign loans in recent years shows that Austria, Bulgaria, Hungary, Roumania, and Yugo-Slavia have absorbed an important proportion of the accommodation granted. French interests therefore coincide fundamentally with our own in respect of any measures initiated for the purpose of assisting a recovery in Central Europe, and in regard to the wider question of monetary policy designed to raise the general level of world prices. It would, therefore, appear that a settlement of the vexed reparations problem would open the way to a common purpose in the monetary policies of the two great financial centres, London and Paris, such as unhappily has been sadly lacking in latter years.

AMERICA

Whereas the French reaction to the financial crisis has manifested itself in an effort to secure the repatriation

THE EXTERNAL SITUATION

of funds deposited abroad, in America the main endeavour has concentrated upon an attempt to secure a reversal of the apparently unending downward trend of commodity prices. Unfortunately the abandonment of the gold standard by Great Britain and those who followed caused a further severe fall (vide Appendix).

The belief is widely held in America, and possibly with truth, that the home market in itself is adequate to secure a return of prosperity granted the requisite conditions. Hitherto the atmosphere has been so charged with depression as to paralyse all efforts to resuscitate confidence.

For a due appreciation of America's difficulties it is necessary to realize that the relative change in her circumstances is greater than that of any other country. The buoyancy and confidence which accompanied a greater material prosperity than has ever before been achieved by any nation in history, has given place to the pessimism and inertia inculcated by an utterly unlooked for adversity, far exceeding that of this country. The unexpectedness of the reverse accentuates both the psychological reaction and the practical difficulties. There are no precise figures which make it possible to say definitely the present number of the unemployed in America: it is estimated to be more than ten millions. This in itself is an immense social problem which came upon America while she was quite unprepared. For although official opinion is against what is called the "dole" system, the alternative of voluntary charity and a hastily improvised organization would, prima facie, appear quite unequal to a satisfactory discharge of the task involved.

Another pressing cause of anxiety has been the failure of a very large number of the smaller banking institutions—more than 3,600 out of some 26,000 in the past two years. These concerns have operated to serve the needs of particular districts somewhat after the manner of the "country banks" in an earlier period of British history. Their failure has largely been brought about by "frozen credit" advances, by actual insolvency of customers, and by security depreciation. The main banking structure of America has not been endangered by these failures, but naturally a great deal of alarm as to the safety of subsidiary institutions has been caused among the general public. This has led to the hoarding of bank notes on a sufficient scale to occasion uneasiness in financial circles. Special measures were designed to meet the hoarding menace in the shape of "baby-loans," i.e. loans inviting subscription of small sums of $10 and upwards guaranteed by the Treasury and bearing interest at 2 per cent. By this means it was hoped to tempt the hoarder to invest his money. Measures were also adopted for restoring the liquidity of the banks and these proved a more effective specific.

On the condition of trade itself the available statistics speak only too eloquently. Overseas trade in 1931 was lower than any year since 1914. The following are the figures:

THE EXTERNAL SITUATION

(In Million Dollars)

	Exports	Imports
1914	2,113	1,789
1929	5,240	4,399
1930	3,843	3,060
1931	2,423	2,089

Exports to Europe in 1931 comprised 48·9 per cent of the whole as against 47·8 per cent in 1930. Canada came next with 40 per cent. Imports from Europe amounted to 30 per cent of the total, and were also 30 per cent down on the previous year.

In regard to internal trade the experience of the railroads affords depressing testimony. The year 1930 was at the time regarded as one of the worst ever encountered by the railroad companies. Gross earnings fell by over $1,014 million or 15·98 per cent, and net earnings by over $432 million or 24·02 per cent. In 1931, however, additional losses of almost equal severity were sustained, the gross fall being over $1,105 million or 20·71 per cent and the net $395 million or 28·94 per cent. The gross fall from 1929 to 1931 was thus from $6·3 billion to $4·2 billion. Even the strongest companies were consequently compelled to reduce or pass dividends.

The special circumstances of the outlying banks and the railroads dictated the form of the measures adopted to relieve the general situation. Thus the Reconstruction Finance Corporation with a potential capital of $2,000 million,[1] of which $500 million is guaranteed by the

---

[1] Since increased by $1,500 million.

State, was especially framed to enable railroad companies to obtain capital on reasonable terms, in order that they might embark on electrification and other schemes of improvement with attendant contracts to industry at large. The companies were invited to apply direct to the Corporation for loans not exceeding $100 million to any one company, and for a period not exceeding three years, the assumption being, of course, that at the expiration of the three-year term conditions will be sufficiently restored for the raising of long-term capital loans in the ordinary way.

The scope of the Corporation's activities is, however, not limited to any special sphere. A large number of financial institutions were advised that loans for up to a three-year period would be available to them for financing agricultural, commercial, and industrial enterprise. Loans made in this manner would be against the promissory notes of the borrowing house or by way of rediscounting obligations tendered for the purpose.

It remains to be seen what measure of success will attend this scheme, but the underlying conception appears to be sound; losses will no doubt be incurred, but the gains should outweigh them.

The help offered to the banks has been through the agency of certain amendments to the Federal Reserve Act incorporated in a Bank Credit Act, the general object of which is to broaden the basis of credit for the emergency period.

THE EXTERNAL SITUATION

One of the most important changes is that relating to the issue of Federal Reserve Notes. Prior to the new Act these notes were covered by gold to the extent of 40 per cent, the remaining 60 per cent being represented by commercial bills. By the amended regulations the gold backing of 40 per cent is retained, but for the further 60 per cent it is permitted to utilize United States Government obligations. Although the legal gold backing is thus unaltered the amendment sets free gold held as cover in excess of 40 per cent. The excess gold was estimated by Senator Carter Glass, a proponent of the measure, to amount to $800 million.[1] This section of the Act is designed to relieve the banks of any embarrassment resulting from further withdrawals of gold on foreign account and to provide an alternative supply for the deficiency in commercial bills caused by the decline in trade.

A further clause in the new Act, which has been subjected to considerable criticism, is that which enables a group of not less than five member banks to obtain advances from the Federal Reserve Bank. These advances may be made subject to the approval of five members of the Federal Reserve Board on the ground that the group has otherwise no adequate or acceptable assets, such as would have enabled sufficient accommodation to be obtained under previously existing legislation. No specific requirement is laid down as to the security

[1] It is probably nearer $1,000 million.

necessary in order to obtain accommodation of this kind, the phrase employed being "such collateral security as may be agreed upon." But it is significant that foreign Government bonds are specially excluded as eligible collateral.

A temporary emergency clause grants still wider powers to the Federal Reserve Banks. Under "exceptional and exigent circumstances" it allows a member bank with a capital not exceeding $5,000,000, and without otherwise eligible assets, to obtain credit facilities from the Reserve Bank on the borrowing bank's time or promissory note secured to the satisfaction of the Reserve Bank. This provision is made applicable for one year only, to March 3, 1933.

There is no doubt that procedure of this kind for the free creation of credit demands careful and strict supervision. The permission to employ United States Government obligations as 60 per cent backing for notes, further emphasizes the need, if such were required, for strict budgetary control and equilibrium. The freedom granted the Federal Reserve Board in fixing the collateral to be accepted from borrowing banks places considerable responsibility on those bodies to avoid an undue proportion of secondary and possibly non-liquid assets. There is no ground, however, for assuming that the responsibility will not be fully recognized and due precaution observed.

The Federal Reserve Bank authorities have meantime accepted the new facilities as furthering their policy of deliberate credit expansion designed to reverse the continued downward movement of prices. The plan adopted is for the Reserve Banks to purchase Government Securities with steady consistency, which they have done for some months past.[1] The object of these purchases is to increase the deposits of Member Banks with the Reserve Banks. Such deposits being treated by the former as cash, serve to broaden the basis upon which further credit can be created.

So far, however, the expansion of credit has been used mainly to offset the outflow of gold, and to reduce the indebtedness of the Member Banks to the Reserve System—the Member Banks having been obliged to borrow heavily during the hoarding epidemic. That the new credit has not gone into circulation is due to the absence of trade demand in the unpropitious conditions ruling. These were such that an immediate trade response was highly improbable. The efficacy of the expansionist policy depends upon a cheap and plentiful supply of credit being assured to industry over a prolonged period.

GERMANY

In no country has the fateful latter half of 1931 produced such far-reaching modifications of the economic system as in Germany. In brief, the effect has been to

---

[1] A reference to the Statistical Appendix will provide evidence of the extent to which the policy has been applied.

suspend free economic action and to transform the country into the most closely controlled State supervised organism outside Russia.

The transformation has been dictated by the pressure of events. When the two great banks, the Danatbank and the Dresdner Bank, failed, immediate action was demanded to prevent calamity overtaking the entire banking and financial system. The liabilities of the banks were guaranteed, but this in itself was not a sufficient and final solution. Both the existing position and subsequent events called for a widening of the area of control until, eventually, the whole price structure was no longer the expression of natural economic forces, but rather the subject of the limitations and modifications of State decree.

After guaranteeing the banks' depositors the next step was to make arrangements to provide facilities for the acceptance and discount of bills for industrial concerns. For this purpose an Acceptance and Guarantee Bank was established. The foreign exchange system was subjected to close control in order to prevent a collapse caused by the calling in of claims on foreign account and a flight of capital on home account. The exchange control was not only strict, but was tightened from month to month. German nationals were instructed to register their holdings of foreign exchange and foreign bonds and shares at the Reichsbank. The owners of foreign exchange if called upon were required to sell their holdings to the Reichsbank at the official rate. The sale of foreign Stock Exchange securities has not so far been demanded; but the income in foreign currency must be sold to the Reichsbank.

Special arrangements were made to secure the repatriation of exported capital. A tax amnesty was offered to those who had set up special funds abroad to escape taxation, enabling them to apply for a special internal loan and to secure immunity from further proceedings. Trust funds held abroad if not repatriated within the prescribed period were made subject to special penal taxation. The crime of "flight from taxation" was established, which imposes penalties on persons leaving the country without sanction between the dates March 31, 1931, and January 1, 1933.

At the beginning of September negotiations were successfully completed to stabilize the indebtedness to foreign banks by a "standstill agreement" postponing the recall of funds, and since extended.

Unfortunately the difficulties besetting Germany were considerably accentuated by the decision of Great Britain to revoke the gold standard. Previous disastrous experience with a paper currency wrought public apprehension to a pitch which made it impossible for Germany to follow suit. The Government was therefore compelled to adopt a diametrically opposite policy to that of England and to meet depreciated exchange with lowered prices. A comprehensive emergency decree on

December 5th compulsorily reduced all prices by at least 10 per cent. The office of "Price Commissioner" was established to supervise the scheme and prevent the prices of essential commodities from rising. In order to make price reduction possible it was necessary to provide for a reduction in the constituent elements of producers' costs. Wages and salaries were reduced by not more than 10 per cent compared with January 1927; Rents by 10 per cent compared with the pre-War level; Mortgage bonds upon a basis that assumed a basic level of 6 per cent. Bonds carrying interest between 6 per cent and 8 per cent were in future to bear interest at 6 per cent, with a schedule of reduction for higher rates. The rate of bank interest and that on all long-term debts except foreign obligations was also reduced.

The condition of the Reich finances precluded the possibility of making corresponding reductions in taxation. The depression in trade reduced the yield of taxation, the more so since an important source of revenue is the levy on the receipts of wage-earners. Earnings were diminished in amount by the provisions of the decree, and the number earning by growing unemployment. In one important direction taxation was increased, namely, in respect of the turnover tax, which was raised from 2 per cent to $2\frac{1}{2}$ per cent—a regrettable necessity as tending to counteract measures designed to reduce prices.

The crux of the question now is whether industry

THE EXTERNAL SITUATION

can continue to function under the measures introduced and in face of the universal contraction of trade. The current situation is one of extreme difficulty. This condition is of course reflected in an increase in the number of persons unemployed, which had reached the appalling total of over six million persons in March 1932.

An analysis of the percentages of unemployment in particular trades[1] is even more impressive than the total. At the end of January 1932 the percentage of trade union unemployed was 44·4 per cent. The Textile Workers' Union reported 45·2 per cent, the Woodworkers' 64 per cent. In the seasonal trades even these rates were eclipsed. The Builders' Trade Unions showed 88 per cent out of work, Carpenters' 88·8, Stonemasons' 89·1, Painters' 89·7 per cent.

The average wage level was 9·6 per cent lower on January 1, 1932, than December 1, 1931.

German policy has so far been firmly directed towards maintaining interest payments on German loans abroad, in particular the Dawes and Young loans. The necessary foreign exchange has been obtained as the result of the export surplus which attained considerable dimensions in 1931, but only at the price of rigid curtailment of imports, the export total being lower than for the previous year.

The recent tariff regulations are intended to reinforce this policy by the virtual exclusion of certain imports,

[1] The writer is indebted to *The Statist* for the figures subsequently quoted.

the duties on which have been raised tenfold and may lead other countries to conclude trade treaties as an alternative to retaliatory measures. As was anticipated by the Basle Bankers Committee, the German export surplus is now diminishing, and unless the tendency is reversed it is difficult to see how the exchange necessary for the service of funded obligations abroad is to be obtained. The scanty reserves of the Reichsbank have been further drawn upon since the beginning of the year.

The gravity of the German position is plain enough. Indeed, it is impossible to withhold recognition of the fortitude of the German public in face of an economic trial of unparalleled severity. All classes are still passing through a fierce ordeal. It would seem that only an early alleviation of the economic situation can save Germany from a social and political upheaval of the first order.

THE DANUBIAN COUNTRIES

The painful trial through which Germany is passing is unfortunately paralleled, if not intensified, in several other countries of Central and Eastern Europe. The plight of Austria and Hungary is nothing less than pitiful. Czecho-Slovakia, Poland, and the Balkan States are all struggling desperately with the problems set up by extreme depression. Imports are reduced to a minimum. Everywhere trade continues to contract—especially international trade. The new countries exporting chiefly primary commodities suffer from the depression of their customers. Prices remain at the lowest levels and consequently the burden of debts becomes intolerable. To secure the funds necessary to pay interest foreign exchange is rationed. The embargoes on exchange further contract trade and thus the vicious reactions spread.

When the world's most powerfully organized nations have been reduced to such a parlous state by the slump it is not surprising that the plight of the Danubian countries (a convenient designation for the countries of Central and South-Eastern Europe) should be wellnigh desperate. For it is generally recognized that the statesmen who formulated the Peace Treaties which delimited the boundaries of these countries were preoccupied with political considerations, and devoted very little time to the economic implications of their arrangements, or the prospects of the new countries being able to secure a reasonable degree of prosperity in the turmoil of the post-War world.

Certainly the Succession States themselves, somewhat intoxicated as they have been by the realization of their nationalist aspirations, have done little towards promoting a workable trade relationship. On the contrary each has been engaged in a preposterous attempt to secure a large measure of economic self-sufficiency. A simple illustration will demonstrate the absurdity of the results.

The export trade of Austria and Czecho-Slovakia

alone of the Danubian countries consists predominantly of manufactured goods: in both cases it amounts to over 70 per cent of the total. In Bulgaria and Yugo-Slavia the proportion is below 10 per cent, and while exact figures are not available in the case of Greece and Roumania, it is probable that the same proportion applies to them both. As regards Hungary the percentage is about 20 per cent. Yet both Austrian and Czech manufacturers in order to obtain a footing in the markets of their neighbours, and despite the limited manufacturing capacity of the latter, have to overcome a stiff tariff barrier. The position is exactly reversed in respect of agricultural products. The two manufacturing countries have endeavoured to supply a large part of their cereal requirements from within their own borders. Such a policy could only become feasible by the imposition of lofty customs duties on equivalent foreign imports. The extent to which these have been imposed can be imagined from the fact that the price of wheat in these countries has been raised to two and even three times that prevailing in Hungary and Roumania, countries which, of course, are natural wheat-growing areas. A further consequence of this unfortunate policy is the emergence of agrarian parties in Austria and Czecho-Slovakia who, being dependent for their existence on the maintenance of tariffs, are naturally strongly opposed to any schemes which suggest the need of their reduction.

THE EXTERNAL SITUATION

A group of countries founded on such an unstable economic basis was clearly in no case to encounter the fierce adversity of the slump, involving as it did a tremendous fall in world prices. Recently a report on the financial position of Austria, Bulgaria, Greece and Hungary was prepared by the Financial Committee of the League of Nations. It was pointed out that although Bulgaria actually succeeded in increasing her exports in 1930 by 80 per cent in weight, yet the monetary value declined by 3 per cent. In 1931 the weight was increased by a further 40 per cent. But the money proceeds were lower still by 4 per cent.

Taking the position of these countries as a whole it was estimated that as a consequence of the fall in prices, the burden of debt-charges on producers of raw material and foodstuffs had increased by no less than 70 per cent. Thus the debtor countries in order to meet interest payments are called upon to sell abroad a 70 per cent larger proportion of their products. But as a result of the general contraction in trade the demand for such products from their foreign customers has on the whole substantially diminished. Therefore the debtor countries are physically unable to provide themselves with foreign currency in sufficient amount to enable them to discharge their obligations.

Even before the collapse in world prices the instability of the Danubian position, like that of Germany, was only obscured by an influx of foreign capital, mostly

American and British. Now, when the need for further capital is more pressing than it has ever been, the credit of these countries is destroyed, so that the League of Nations Financial Committee could suggest no way by which further funds could be provided, except that the lending countries should themselves guarantee the interest on the loans granted. But clearly the provision of loans on any such terms is unthinkable unless, as a prior condition, a workable economic system is established in the recipient countries. Such a conclusion means that for the moment attempts to secure a discharge of existing debt dues must be subordinated to the broader requirements of reconstruction.

Here there emerges into view the underlying community of interest which alone can resolve the present tangle of opposing policies. At present differences amongst the Great Powers themselves as well as domestic and external disharmonies in the States immediately concerned impede every attempted advance.

The interests of Britain, France and America are largely financial. Loans previously granted, however, can only be permanently salvaged by the restoration of a workable trading relationship. This objective seems impossible of attainment apart from a recognition of the important trade interests of Germany and Italy in the Danubian countries.

The Danubian States on their part must expect to make concessions to the plain requirements of economic sanity as a precedent condition to further capital accommodation. Nothing in the nature of a free-trade system is practical politics, but a system of commercial treaties and preferences is both practicable and essential.

The supremely difficult but not hopeless task which confronts international statesmanship in the near future is to bring this tripartite principle of reconstruction into the foreground. Only by according it full recognition can the common welfare of all parties be promoted.

The effort to persuade the Governments and peoples of the world to see their present trials not only in their individual incidence but as part of a great universal disorder makes painfully slow progress. So far they have been content to adopt merely insular expedients which intensify difficulties beyond their own borders to the ultimate detriment of all alike. There is grave danger that a maintenance of this mentality will cause a widening of the area of insolvency and default and so produce further financial calamities.

CHAPTER V

OUTLINES OF A CONSTRUCTIVE SOLUTION

A statistical analysis of the present situation would in itself provide insufficient evidence on which to base belief in an early revival. Here and there some hopeful factor is reported, but the current statistics relating to world trade and the continued throttling effects of foreign exchange embargoes, certainly throw doubt upon the ability of an incipient improvement to outweigh so heavy a burden. Assuredly there seems to be still less reason for supposing that the position in the ultra depressed countries makes them ripe for inherent recovery.

Nor can it fail to strike the observant onlooker that most of the so-called remedies for our existing ills are merely methods for securing sectional advantage. Tariffs, for example, merely erect a barrier to sales by other countries, which as a general measure defeats its own object. Rather than provide the nationals of country X with foreign exchange, enabling them to purchase goods country Y can manufacture more cheaply than X, the people of Y prefer to make for themselves what could be bought more cheaply in X.

A depreciated currency, on the other hand, is simply a device for underselling one's neighbours.

OUTLINES OF A CONSTRUCTIVE SOLUTION

Tariffs beget currency depreciation, and the latter tariffs.

The process known as "getting liquid"[1] provides a further illustration. Obviously it is not one which prevents depreciation of either Stock Exchange values or commodity prices; on the contrary the more widespread the movement the heavier the depreciation. If insisted upon *à l'outrance* by the whole community it would carry prices to zero. To some extent the same reasoning applies to cutting costs and restricting output. There is clearly no alternative to cutting costs—mainly involving a saving on wages both in numbers employed and rates of payment—when the price level is falling and therefore the money value of the output is diminished. But wage payments in themselves constitute the most important element in consumers' demand, which being reduced causes a further fall in prices and the need for still greater economies.

The position is similar in respect of restriction of output. There is no alternative when trade as a whole is contracting; but the marketing of a diminished output involves a contraction of reciprocal demand.

Such measures in themselves so far from constituting a remedy lead finally to inevitable collapse. Wage earnings and price levels interact upon each other to reduce the volume of trade and increase the ratio which

[1] Building up cash deposits or holdings of gilt-edged securities by the sale of lower-grade securities, stocks of commodities, or other assets.

fixed charges bear to the money value of trade sales, until a financial crisis is brought about. A financial crisis itself, as the world has discovered to its cost, is a compound of hurtful reactions. So much so that, despite great stress and much wreckage suffered in recent experience, society, as a whole, may count itself fortunate to have escaped a collapse involving much wider devastation.

If there were no other factors to take into account it might seem that every attempt at restoration was frustrated from the outset. Fortunately the situation is not so bad as that. The real task is to get to the root of the disturbance and discover the possibilities of a constructive solution.

This is the field of monetary theory into which it will be necessary to make a brief incursion in the endeavour to indicate the broad outlines of constructive monetary policy. Monetary policy, because this *is* the root of the matter. "Booms and slumps are simply the expression of the results of an oscillation of the terms of credit about their equilibrium position."[1]

THE ROOT OF THE MATTER

In a collectivist state the producer and purchaser are in identity and there can thus be no disequilibrium between

---

[1] J. M. Keynes, *Treatise on Money*.

OUTLINES OF A CONSTRUCTIVE SOLUTION

production and demand. Under an individualist régime, however, the main part of its economic problems is due to the difficulty confronting the whole body of producers in estimating in advance the future conditions of demand as to taste and tendency—reacting on particular prices—and those of the monetary factors which determine the level of prices in general.

The former aspect does not concern us. On the latter it should be possible to throw some light in summarizing the main outline of the exegesis contained in Mr. J. M. Keynes's *Treatise on Money*.

The community, as a whole, can be viewed at any one time in its capacity of producer of the total stock of goods and services which enter into business relations, and on the other hand in its complementary capacity of complete consumer. The monetary aspects of this fact may be expressed by saying that Total Costs of Production and Consumers' Earnings are the same thing looked at from opposite points of view. There is another element which must be visualized, however, and that is Profits, which may be defined as something more—or in the case of Losses something less—than the minimum anticipated standard of inducement or remuneration necessary to cause the entrepreneur or leader of industry to function.

The consumers' total earnings, that is to say, the incomes of all individuals in the community, are apportioned between expenditure on consumption goods and savings. Producers' costs, on the other hand, are apportioned between that part of costs which is absorbed in bringing to market goods directly available for consumption and that part expended in producing "non-available" goods; that is, fixed capital goods and goods "in process." It is obvious that if consumers devote the same proportion of their total earnings to expenditure on consumption goods as producers have devoted to bringing them to market, the price level of consumption goods will be stable.

Whether this correlation is actually achieved depends in turn on the maintenance of a correspondence between the proportion of consumers' income devoted to saving and the proportion of industrial costs devoted to the production of non-available goods, i.e. to industrial investment.

If, owing to increased saving, consumers are spending a smaller proportion of their earnings on consumption goods than the proportion of costs devoted by producers to preparing them for sale, the price of consumption goods will fall and producers will not receive back their costs, i.e. they will make a loss. On the other hand, if producers devote a larger percentage of their total costs to industrial investment while the percentage of consumers' savings is unchanged, the price of consumption goods will rise and the producers of these goods will make a profit—or a windfall profit if that term is more clear.

OUTLINES OF A CONSTRUCTIVE SOLUTION

The relation between Savings[1] and Investment is that between Source and Destination though without any necessary time-lag. Saving can occur without Investment. It matters naught how the individual disposes of his unspent income as long as it does not synchronize with a like amount of industrial investment by an entrepreneur. During the financial scare, for example, savings were welcome, and highly remunerated as bank deposits, offsetting the credit deflation in progress. Consumers' savings are not the only source of Investment, since the latter may be reinforced by Profits—or diminished by Losses.

It will be clear that though the connecting-link between Savings and Industrial Investment is the rate of interest it establishes no natural or automatic harmony between their respective requirements.

On the contrary, the more attractive the deposit rate offered for savings the more deterrent is the charge for industrialists' loans and bank credit. In a period of crisis —provided the depositor is confident of the safety of his bank—there is no need for him to trouble further. The promise of a fair rate of interest and no risk precisely meets his requirements. In the business world the situation is quite otherwise: owing to increased risk and diminished profit there is no incentive to undertake further investment.

[1] Excluding the fact that one person's saving may be another's expenditure.

The application of savings, therefore, is determined in the light of two considerations: risk and reward. Differences in temperament and circumstances will create variations in the relative importance attached to each factor, but it is safe to say that the smaller the risk and the greater the remuneration, the better the wishes of the saver will be served.

Industrial investment on its part is entered upon according to the forecast made of the anticipated return to the capital expended. The return to this expenditure is in the form of goods, so that an assumed price level of the product is an essential element in the calculation.

Against the estimated money value of the product must be set the cost of remunerating the other factors of production. The prospective residuum, if any, will then be related to the cost of obtaining the use of fresh capital —i.e. in general, the effective rate of interest. Only if the inducement is adequate will further capital be employed.

The aim of monetary policy disclosed by this analysis is to establish a correspondence between the volume of savings and the value of new investment. Needless to say, an exact balance is impossible of achievement, but as a mean above and below which the actual proportions employed fluctuate, the banking system by varying the price and quantity of bank credit can exercise ultimate control. The maintenance of this harmonious relationship, it will be observed, will at the same time promote

OUTLINES OF A CONSTRUCTIVE SOLUTION

general stability of the price level by equating the relative proportions of expenditure and costs devoted to consumption goods by consumer and producer respectively.

Special attention should be directed towards the role marked out for the producer of capital goods by the operation of the monetary mechanism. A deficiency in industrial investment will react upon the demand for the products of the makers of fixed-capital goods, and will cause them to contract their operations. The resulting depression and severe unemployment will lead to a decline in consumers' demand as a reflection of the depression in those industries. The outcome of the further fall in prices will be to reduce the return to industrial effort and to further diminish the confidence of the saving community, thus enlarging the gap dividing their interests.

Every observer of the economic situation recognizes that it is the latter form of depression, due to famine in industrial investment or demand for capital goods, from which the world is now suffering.

It is equally apparent that the conditions of trade revival are, first, a diminution in the rates offered on bank deposits and gilt-edged investment, the other aspect of which is a reduction in the charges made to industry for capital accommodation; and, secondly, a restoration of the price level which will increase the money value of the product.

As regards capital goods the two things go together, since a reduction in interest charges so operates that it raises the demand price for capital goods. That is, the price at which it just pays the industrialist to purchase capital goods. Theoretically, the demand price is increased to the extent of the capitalized value of the change in the long-term borrowing rate. Thus, if a reduction of 1 per cent in the bank-rate causes a $\frac{1}{4}$ per cent fall in the long-term rate and, therefore, a 5 per cent rise in the market price of prime industrial debentures, other things being equal, it will increase by the latter percentage the demand price of capital goods.

The demand price for consumption goods does not necessarily move in conjunction with that of capital goods, as will be clear when it is reflected that it would pay an industrialist to employ capital at 4 per cent to effect a 5 per cent reduction in costs, even though the movement in the price of consumption goods might be downward. Nevertheless, as a general rule, the prices of the two classes of goods will move together. A demand for capital goods at the present time would bring contracts to some depressed industries, which would lead to an expansion of employment and an increase in wage-earnings. Thus the demand for consumption goods would be restored and thereafter the general price level. These by previous analysis we know to be precisely the conditions essential to revival.

OUTLINES OF A CONSTRUCTIVE SOLUTION

GROUNDS FOR HOPE

We have reached a point at which it should be clear that the root of our troubles in recent years is the abuse to which the monetary system has been subjected, and that, accordingly, their solution must be sought in the same sphere. The ultimate desiderata of monetary policy have been plain for some time past. The hopeful feature is that events are shaping themselves in such a way that many obstacles have already been overcome. The necessities of the case are plainer every day, and must ere long overcome what recalcitrance remains.

When a depression is in full course it cannot be checked merely by a policy of credit expansion. While prices are falling severely there is no prospect of new production realizing a margin over costs. A cheap credit policy under such circumstances would need to be reinforced by a concerted buying movement to check the fall. If a period of financial alarm issues from the depression, control of the situation can, as a rule, only be regained by the vigorous use of the bank-rate designed to check withdrawals and speed up repayment of advances. Until fears have subsided, expansive measures would be suicidal; but when calm has returned and prices have steadied, the time for curative action is opportune.

A better opportunity is now afforded of reversing the long-drawn-out process of deflation than has been perceptible at any time since the slump occurred, owing to the fact that the destructive forces appear to have been sapped of much of their power.

The dear-money disturbance of the Wall Street boom has long since passed. The subsequent stock-market slump has probably run its course. Reparation payments are not likely in future to occupy a place of such importance in international exchange as to form an impediment to world progress. The capital withdrawals movement has been carried almost to its practicable limits; or at any rate funds not already called in are apparently presumed to be safe where they are, or are simply immobilized. It is true that owing to the fall in prices the existing burden of debts is well-nigh intolerable for many countries, and a widening of the area of default is an imminent danger which can by no means be overlooked. It can only be hoped that the obvious straits of some of the smaller countries may stir the big creditor nations to concerted constructive action. The real remedy in this respect can only come from success in treating the general problem of the world price level. It is in this direction that grounds for new hope are discernible. In this country and the large group of countries which have abandoned gold it should be possible by appropriate monetary action not only to avoid a further fall in prices, but to encourage an upward movement. In this group there is now opportunity for the expression of a more intelligent monetary policy than one which is ordered merely by the desire to conserve a scanty

OUTLINES OF A CONSTRUCTIVE SOLUTION

stock of gold. The root conditions of industrial recovery can therefore be fulfilled. The mere availability of cheap credit facilities, it is true, will not prove effective over a short term; supplementary measures, as will be shown, are likely to be necessary. But its influence should not be underestimated. At the present time there are many thousands of millions of pounds value of various currencies lying on short-term deposit in the chief monetary centres throughout the world. The owners of the greater part of this vast accumulation have been under no desire or compulsion to find a permanent investment outlet for their funds, in view of the comparatively high rate of remuneration they have hitherto been offered for allowing their balances to remain liquid.

The requirements of the position call for a reduction in the bank-rate to, say, 2 per cent, with a corresponding reduction in short-term rates.[1] This will cause a large body of capital to seek higher remuneration in productive employment. For the industrial interests to receive any benefit it is of course necessary that the reduction of short-term rates shall be followed by an equivalent movement in the long-term or bond rate of interest. In our own country this objective would be facilitated by success attending the efforts of the Treasury in converting to a lower interest basis (as they undoubtedly intend) the immense mass of £2,000 million 5 per cent War Loan, 1929–47. The continued existence

[1] Since the above was written it is gratifying to have observed considerable progress in this direction.

of this huge amount of Government guaranteed stock bearing a comparatively high rate of interest must inevitably prove, while it remains, a substantial barrier to a material reduction of industrial interest rates.

An economy of under twenty million pounds per annum on the interest service for this loan would be a small matter by comparison with the consequences which would follow in enabling other Governments and industrial undertakings to replace some of their most burdensome debt by loans, debentures, etc., raised on easier terms.

Further, a fall in the bond or long-term interest rate leading to a rise in security values, at first confined to gilt-edged stocks, but afterwards, from the attraction of the higher return offered, spreading to other investment securities, would operate to correct the present debilitated demand by reducing the tendency to over-saving which is the concomitant of a falling market—a tendency which is not only manifested by individuals, but by corporate bodies as many a company report will prove. A relaxation of saving and hoarding would thus tend to "oil the wheels of industry" by stimulating personal and corporate expenditure, the effect of which on the general price might be an important factor.

There still remains the fact that at the existing level of prices, there may be no incentive to increase production.

There are several observations to be made on this aspect of the case. In the first place, as already explained,

OUTLINES OF A CONSTRUCTIVE SOLUTION

the demand for fixed capital goods does not necessarily depend on an existing ability of producers of consumption goods to earn a profit. It is sufficient that the anticipated return to the capital employed should exceed the cost of borrowing. There is thus likely to be a gradual demand for capital among high-grade borrowers, even apart from an early corrective of the disparity between costs and prices. This demand, not being confined to any one country, will tend to unlock the capital market to credit-worthy borrowers in overseas countries, and thus will promote a revival of international trade among countries linked together by the sterling exchange.

The resumption of capital loan operations by the creditor countries is of fundamental importance. The heart of the difficulty which has to be faced is that the severity of the slump has been such that but few solvent borrowers are left. In less desperate circumstances it is not necessary to supply fresh capital in quarters where prima facie the need is greatest. For this reason: if capital can be usefully employed in any particular centre, the increased activity in that area will furnish a supply of orders to places and industries far removed from the source of origin; thus by affording capital accommodation to sound borrowers the risk is diminished and the benefit spreads outward.

In so far as such borrowers exist at the present time the same considerations apply, but there is no doubt that special treatment will be required to meet the present extreme situation. The creditor countries will be compelled to take in hand a reconstruction programme, whether they like it or not. The common adversity will at length compel co-operation; *force majeure* will prove more convincing advocacy than the suasions of pure reason. In the years following the post-War slump, the leading European creditor countries, by means of the agency of the League of Nations, effected several reconstruction schemes—in one case that of Austria, by means of the lending countries guaranteeing the service of a loan. The experience of investors in many other loans has been so disastrous that apart from a somewhat similar guarantee it is impossible to imagine that the public would respond to invitations to subscribe. Hitherto, reconstruction measures of this kind have almost exclusively taken the form of loans to the Governments concerned, and as a consequence whenever default has occurred the investor has found that he has neither security nor hopeful recourse of any kind. It is at least worthy of consideration whether the same purpose might not be achieved—concurrently with a scheme for stabilization of their national finances—by granting credit facilities to sound and substantial business undertakings against tangible collateral—such as mortgages, suitably guaranteed debentures, etc., which should be mobilized and held by a finance corporation created for the purpose. Such a scheme would partake of the nature of an International Reconstruction Finance

OUTLINES OF A CONSTRUCTIVE SOLUTION

Corporation on the American model, but adapted to the requirements of international finance.

The capital of the Corporation would be subscribed internationally as in the case of the Bank of International Settlements, who might well operate the scheme. It would be necessary that the Governments of the lending countries should guarantee a part of the capital, the remaining portion being taken up by a group representative of international banking and finance houses, and by the general public. Loans granted should be primarily for the purpose of enabling the borrowers to make external purchases. Such purchases would be paid for in effect by a draft on the funds of the Finance Corporation, which would be covered by the automatic calling up of an equivalent subscription to the Corporation from the banking representatives of the country receiving the order. A scheme of this kind should prove beneficial in two important respects: that of relieving the capital famine in the countries selected for assistance, and in relaxing the extreme stringency characterizing the foreign exchange market. A readier flow of foreign exchange would be of extreme value in re-establishing better conditions in international trade, and would, undoubtedly, serve to promote considerably more business than that represented by the originating transactions.

There can be little doubt that the position of Germany, and those other countries in Europe which are able to adhere to the gold standard only by rigid control of the foreign exchange machinery, would be greatly eased by carrying out a scheme of devaluation. This means that the gold content of the respective currency units of the countries concerned would be diminished. Such a measure would be followed by a fall in the external value of the currency, as represented by the foreign exchange quotations. But as the internal value of the currency, as represented in the cost of living, would be largely unaltered, the trading community would experience a benefit; while the banking system would at all events be partially relieved of the necessity for the rigid restriction and regulation of exchange dealings, which in itself constitutes a barrier to the flow of trade.

Measures of this kind have not hitherto been taken for fear that any attempt to do so would lead to a general panic which would itself cause the development feared, namely, a plunge into the abyss of inflation. It would appear that Germany has now sufficiently strong grasp of the situation to undertake a step of this nature. It would, of course, be greatly facilitated if the co-operation of the central banks of other leading countries was secured in advance.

In some quarters it has been recommended that the policy of devaluation should be undertaken by all the gold-standard countries, and thus set free a very considerable sum of reserve gold. If a part of these reserves was handed over to an international central

OUTLINES OF A CONSTRUCTIVE SOLUTION

bank, of the nature referred to in the succeeding chapter, important benefits would accrue. The need for the actual transfer of gold between one country and another to settle uncovered debts would be largely diminished. A few book entries to the debit of the bank of one country and the credit of the bank of another in the accounts of the supernational bank would suffice to make the necessary adjustments. In this way the present stock of gold would "go further." Moreover, a stimulus would be given to the future production of gold since a given weight of the metal would be worth more in commodities. These effects are of great importance in view of the possibility of a gold shortage in subsequent years.

A plan of this kind is obviously dependent upon international agreement, which takes time to secure. In the meantime it may well be that efforts to discover a deliberate constructive solution of present difficulties may be assisted by spontaneous developments on the part of industry itself. Previous experience points to the almost infinite adaptability with which by technological improvements and inventions society meets every new situation. In some section of industry such innovations are likely to disclose a profit margin where none exists to-day, and the improving tendency in one trade will beneficially react on others.

It is the combination of factors such as those outlined that at last will check the long decline of trade and prices and set up a forward movement. There is ground for thinking that a change of mind among merchants and manufacturers under such circumstances would suffice to bridge the gap between current costs and prices. Costs have already been largely accommodated to the existing level of prices, while the further accumulation of stocks is slow, despite the markedly subnormal condition of trade demand. A broad movement for the replenishment of stocks now depleted to their fullest extent by the prolonged decline would be sufficient to cause a sharp improvement in prices, and if associated with curative measures of the nature described would mark the turning of the tide towards prosperity.

The general summing-up of the foregoing argument is as follows: The world has been brought low by its own unreason. The courses pursued inevitably led to a financial crisis. Having wrought less damage than might have been feared this has now been succeeded by a calmer period, which, however, is by no means devoid of threatening circumstances. There is some ground for better hopes of the future in that many of the destructive influences which have previously exercised a powerfully deflationary effect may have largely spent their force. There is reason also for supposing that man's native inventiveness will, given a fair opportunity, do much to accommodate itself to the existing situation. This in itself does not provide sufficient justification for passively awaiting automatic revival, especially as many

OUTLINES OF A CONSTRUCTIVE SOLUTION

countries are still in the grip of the evil consequences of constantly dwindling prices. The trend of events appears happily to have brought the particular interests of countries into greater harmony than has hitherto existed, making it probable that the corrective of universal cheap money will be applied. The hiatus between costs and prices may prove to be no greater than can be bridged by the usual response of prices to a change in sentiment and revival of demand. The latter should be initiated not only by unlocking the capital market by low money rates, but by specific corporate endeavours designed to alleviate the difficulties of the specially depressed countries.

SOME PRACTICAL IMPLICATIONS AND RESERVATIONS

It will perhaps be well to offer some observations on the practical business implications of the opinions that have been expressed.

The investing public are now witnessing the first effects of cheap money in the substantial advancement of gilt-edged securities—a movement which may be expected to go further if financial disturbances due to the plight of the most seriously affected countries can be avoided. It would not be surprising if borrowers of the first order offering $4\frac{1}{2}$ per cent to 5 per cent take the precaution of inserting clauses which give a right of redemption at comparatively near dates.

These may not suit the average investor, who will

want to be assured of the rate of return currently offered over a longer period. He will perhaps be well advised therefore to choose long-dated securities obtainable at below or near par. But since the maintenance of low-interest rates cannot be counted upon after trade becomes active, the value of a redemption date ensuring the repayment of the capital sum on a specific date at a fixed price should by no means be ignored. The beginnings of recovery will probably be accompanied by invitations to the public to subscribe for various issues ranking in the secondary or lower grades of credit. These are likely to be sufficiently numerous to offer a wide choice to investors and to check the upward progress of first-grade stocks.

It is necessary to offer a word of warning lest any suggestion of impending recovery may serve as a stimulus to unwise investment—particularly in ordinary shares. General considerations—such as that makers of constructional material, shipbuilders, and the like, should have most to gain from a business revival—are apt to be more dangerous than useful, apart from a careful estimation of the individual merits of each concern. Nevertheless, the probabilities certainly justify the view that the ordinary or common shares of established undertakings are in many cases undervalued in relation to what may be regarded as normal earning capacity.

As regards business generally, "discriminatory enter-

OUTLINES OF A CONSTRUCTIVE SOLUTION

prise" might well be adopted as a watchword. Economy needs to be distinguished from inertia. Undertakings with sufficient capital to utilize the present period for effecting improvements and modernizing their organization by proceeding accordingly may well be acting wisely for themselves as well as in the common interest. The danger is that the widespread economy campaign may strangle enterprise and development which in themselves would be vindicated by results.

The existing level of commodity prices would also seem to justify a more liberal attitude than the hand-to-mouth dealing which has been inculcated by the prolonged fall in prices. This is not to say that speculative purchases would be desirable from any point of view. In fact, an outbreak of speculation would be particularly dangerous under present conditions, and might endanger the whole scheme of restorative monetary policy. The objective advocated in the Macmillan Report was defined as being first of all "to raise prices a long way above their present level and then to maintain them at the level thus reached with as much stability as can be arranged." If a speculative movement got under weigh it might prove uncontrollable and again set in motion the unfortunate sequence of inflation and deflation. Some substantial upward movement must, however, be accepted as a necessary objective, and that it may be sudden in its early phases should cause neither surprise nor premature alarm. "As soon as business begins to lift its head again we may be sure that austere voices will be raised declaring there is an incipient inflation of credit present which must be scotched, when in fact the existing deflation of prices will not yet have been redressed."

These are the words of the Macmillan Majority Report. Their aim was stated to be "a large rise towards the price level of 1928." There are grounds for thinking that this objective should now be moderated. Adjustments and price contraction that have since occurred suggest that balance might be restored by a more limited advance, while the existence of a paper currency in many countries besides our own calls for cautious procedure.

CHAPTER VI

A WORLD IN TRANSITION

The world has suffered a bitter trial in the past two and a half years: its future well-being greatly depends upon the extent to which it will prove to have profited by experience. Are there any good reasons for supposing that sufficient wisdom and knowledge has been gained from these recent events to place economic functions on a sounder footing than in the past? The tacit assumption of the time is that the question can be answered in the affirmative; there is no need to emphasize the importance of proving its validity by subsequent accomplishment. For it must be clear to all thinking people that the whole nature of the economic problem has been transformed in very recent years. Pre-War economics held one fundamental concept in common with the eighteenth-century writers on political economy—as it was then called. To both of them it seemed beyond question that a state of poverty must inevitably be associated with conditions of dearth and deficiency. The Iron Law of Wages was formulated in the belief that inexorable laws of nature prevented the standard of life of the masses rising much above the bare level of subsistence. Any temporary improvement would only be followed by an increase in population up to the maximum capacity of the soil to sustain life. Even in the period immediately before the War most economists believed that the main obstacle to greater material well-being lay on the supply side of industry, and were therefore concerned with the difficulty of producing a large enough "cake" for everybody to have a good share.

Only of late years has the productive capacity of the community clearly demonstrated its ability to exceed greatly the present standard of consumption. At the present time the American steel industry is working at well below 25 per cent of capacity; and in other industries the difference is only one of degree. The essential nature of the problem of want is thus completely changed. The deficiency to be analysed is not one of supplies but of effective demand. Further progress lies in enabling people to claim products and take them away as fast as the great industrial machine is able to produce them. And since no physical impossibility prevents their doing so, investigation turns its attention to the sphere of distribution and exchange, with attention chiefly concentrated on the latter in an effort to improve the efficiency of the monetary mechanism. Success in this direction would manifest itself in ability to maintain a generally even balance between consumers' expenditure and producers' costs—in other words, in ability to maintain a general stability of the price level. Sir Josiah Stamp has described the problem of the price level as "the most important single problem of the age." When it is recognized that from the monetary phenomenon known as the credit cycle proceed booms and slumps, and from the latter unemployment, social distress, and financial nightmares, the statement will appear as one not to be lightly contradicted.

The trouble is the "inherent instability of credit"—to use Mr. Hawtrey's term. A period of trade revival leads to a demand for increased credit facilities. Taking the position as it exists after a considerable period of depression it is likely that money will be cheap and balances inactive. Then some stimulus to production occurs—perhaps due to the opening up of a new field of enterprise following a new invention. It may be that even an incipient recovery suffices to disclose the current rate of production as being below probable requirements. Activity, therefore, tends to spread outward. Additional employment is offered and wage payments increase. Even at this stage the banking system is a consenting party by expanding the circulation of money and so enabling these payments to be made. The increased circulation of money is so much additional buying power, and thus stimulates the current demand for goods and the pulse of the industrial organism. Opportunities for the profitable employment of further capital may be discerned here and there and the public will thereupon be invited to subscribe for new issues.

The proceeds of these issues will be used in the purchase of goods and probably in employing additional labour. The output in goods of the capital so employed will, however, not come to market until the production period is complete. The price of consumption goods will rise on this account—namely, that consumers' purchasing power is increased without at the same time bringing consumers' goods to market. This affords an additional incentive to producers. Some competition may occur for the services of labour and for goods available for early delivery. The rates of payment offered for each will in that case be raised. The buying movement by this time will be definitely in the ascendant. Producers will be receiving windfall profits and will consequently do their utmost to expand output. Prices, profits, wages and borrowing will be increasing. Why should the process not continue? By reason of the fact that buying power has been allowed to extend more rapidly than the production of the things it purchases. The credit position is thus unsound and will become more so if the movement is allowed to continue. A rise in interest rates is the corrective. This will not only curtail borrowing but cause some selling to repay loans; and, as the previous enlargement of the productive capacity of industry is leading to more goods coming to market, prices will begin to fall. The increased cost of borrowing and the fall in prices will cause industrialists to diminish capital development. With a falling-off in the placing of big contracts the ebb of trade has visibly set in. Lower prices find out the weak spots in the industrial and financial structure. Some people will commence selling because they must, others because they are "bearish" of the outlook. Buyers, on the other hand, will hold off and markets generally will be weak. The manner in which a fall in prices tends to set in motion a general recession to lower and ever lower levels is in the present day a painful commonplace of experience and requires no further description at this stage.

This may be taken as the briefest possible sketch of the credit cycle. It is capable of assuming numberless forms, and its dimensions will be exaggerated or modified according to external conditions. But all are alike in causing trade to fluctuate.

Economists are not agreed in their diagnosis of the nature and inner causes of the credit cycle, nor are they in full accord on the measures required to prevent its recurrence. But even were there complete agreement on underlying principles, their practical application under all conceivable circumstances must necessarily present great difficulties.

Obviously it would require a more than human prescience to make the right decision at any and every given moment. Mistakes, and even serious mistakes, are bound to occur if only for the reason—to employ a cogent American aphorism—that "Hindsight is easier than Foresight." It is easy to see what should have been done when on looking back the relative value of the various components of a given situation have been established. It is quite another matter to rightly appraise them in advance. Take as an example the most glaring of instances: the Wall Street Boom. It was certainly not beyond the power of the monetary machine to check the course of the boom, given a free hand to impose the appropriate deterrent. Some speculators proved their willingness to pay 10 per cent and over for accommodation. It therefore became a matter of charging a rate which would effectively curb such operations. In practice this would not have needed to reach so high a level as 10 per cent, because very dear money in checking the speculator would have damped down trade development also. Here lay the quandary. The majority of people, and many of them experts, did not agree that the situation was unhealthy or required drastic treatment. Even the halting attempts of the banking authorities to regain control of the position aroused much criticism and resentment. Had the whole expansion movement been checked by the autocratic action of a cabal of bankers the entire country would have resounded with the outcry and general condemnation that would have ensued. It must be accepted that in the last resort bankers, no more than statesmen, can resist indefinitely the power of public opinion.

If in this, an extreme example, the authorities were not in agreement, what of the more baffling cases that will every day come up for decision? When one group of commodities is tending to fall and another to rise, as must often be the case, which movement shall be regarded as of the greater importance may very well be a matter of opinion. Moreover, much of the very statistical information on which action is to be determined may be rather a record of past movements than an accurate reflection of existing tendencies.

Nor is this the whole matter. For the right decision of the authorities to be effective they must be in control of a monetary mechanism so organized as to be capable of fully reflecting their intentions. This requirement is probably largely met in this country and in America; but is by no means generally attained. Assuming that the nations of the world will again be linked together by a common standard of value, it is necessary for stability that all the major central banks should be in continuous and effective co-operation. This condition would not be fulfilled while in certain countries the banking mechanism was not responsive to the intention of its authorities. Moreover, co-ordination to be effectively maintained would require the establishment of an International Central Bank, of which the rudimentary organism is to be found in the Bank of International Settlements. An international bank of this kind would perform somewhat similar functions as between the central banks of the chief financial nations to those carried out by a central bank in relation to its member banks. Its value as a stabilizing and co-ordinating factor therefore requires little emphasis. It is to be hoped that any international convention which may be called to discuss world monetary problems will succeed in so broadening the scope of the Bank of International Settlements as to enable it to perform the fundamental functions indicated.

So far it may be thought that a somewhat despondent view of the prospects for a stable monetary system has been presented. This, however, is not intended. In a work of this kind, which is chiefly concerned with the near-at-hand and practical issues, it is necessary to avoid giving a misleading impression of the early prospects. Taking the longer view, however, it is essential to realize that investigation of this aspect of monetary phenomena is only in its infancy. It is only in recent years that the endeavour to maintain a stable price level has been advanced as a cardinal aim of banking practice.[1] Few would doubt that, given workable surrounding conditions—that is, excluding wars, political upheavals, widespread national calamity and the like—sufficient progress has already been made in the art of monetary manipulation to make a considerable measure of success in maintaining price stability a practical possibility, assuming international co-operation and a free hand for the monetary authorities. Success in diminishing the range of fluctuation would be of vital importance,

[1] This is the banking policy recommended by the Macmillan Commission. The stable price level is by no means universally acceptable, however. The reader must be referred to Mr. D. H. Robertson and Professor F. A. von Hayek as prominent among those who hold other views.

because it would mean that the consequent disturbances would be reduced to more manageable proportions and, therefore, become partially amenable to subsidiary correctives of various kinds, such as the dovetailing of public works into the depression intervals.

The proponents of the stable-purchasing-power policy believe it possible to attain this measure of success by means of regulating the volume and terms of bank credit. The central bank's control over the terms of short credit both through the bank-rate and by means of reinforcing measures, such as open-market operations, enables it to exercise a powerful influence on the long-term rate of interest. It has already been shown that upon the long-term or bond rate of interest depends the attractiveness, or otherwise, of producing capital goods, i.e. of industrial investment. An excess or deficiency in the volume of industrial investment relative to the volume of saving determines the rise or fall in the price of consumption goods. If banking policy by changing the terms of bank-credit is competent to control the volume of industrial investment it will thereby be enabled to determine the trend of the general price level. This faculty it will exercise in such a manner as to prevent substantial deviations from the equilibrium level.[1]

It seems probable that on a restoration of more

[1] This level is not a constant, however. A widespread change in methods of production or powerful social forces may cause it to alter. The new equilibrium must then be sought and as far as possible held.

normal conditions banking policy will be shaped towards an effort of this nature, but only time and experience will show to what extent success can be achieved.

From time to time suggestions have been made with a view to diminishing the part of human judgment in taking the decisions which determine credit expansion and contraction. Schemes of this kind are designed to make stabilization automatic. An outstanding example is Professor Irving Fisher's "compensated dollar" based on adjustment of the gold ratio of the currency unit according to the index of the price level, thus releasing gold when prices are falling and reducing reserves when prices are rising. The objection to this scheme, as well as to other automatic currency devices based on an index of price levels, is that it relates credit policy to past events instead of to the future trend. The price index is merely a statistical record of what has already happened.

It is unlikely that much progress will come from proposals of this nature. Monetary management is an art, not an exact science, and must therefore depend on human decision in the light of ever-changing sets of circumstances.

Meanwhile the further potentialities which lie in the progress of monetary science can be appreciated from the fact that a perfect monetary system—though only a theoretical abstraction—would enable producers to operate continuously to capacity and dispose of their output to a body of consumers ever growing in wealth.

A WORLD IN TRANSITION

The world is always hearing of remarkable schemes designed to make this dream a reality, but since people are well aware that currency instability and mental instability are close allied, nobody ever expects anything to accrue from them. Nor are they likely to be wrong. Progress in monetary technique is inevitably a slow evolution marked by growth of knowledge and a gradually perfected mechanism. It would be a profound mistake, however, that scepticism as to an immediate transformation should lead people to despair of any real achievement in the future. For such a view there can be no support. Great strides have been made in recent years; and many brilliant and original thinkers are ever at work pioneering the path to further progress. A more harmonious relationship in international affairs would permit the measure of the advance already made to be demonstrated in the benefit in material well-being of every nation in the world.

THE INDUSTRIAL CONTRIBUTION

In no form of activity is the interval between the germinal idea and its translation into practical effect more pronounced than in that of currency reform. The complexity and breadth of the reactions to monetary changes are such that every suggestion of change demands the utmost scrutiny. The task of the innovator is therefore apt to be a difficult one. Even if he emerges with success from the prolonged theoretical battle, there are still many practical difficulties to overcome: difficulties due to methods of actual working, and the supersession of established custom as well as opposition from quarters where the suggested change is likely to exercise injurious effect.

Thus, in spite of all endeavours, progress in monetary reform must be slow. Industry cannot be content merely to await the outcome, but must seek to find its own means of surmounting the obstacles to its prosperity. In any case, industry is concerned with particular prices as well as with general stability of the price level. Moreover, success in maintaining the average of particular prices is bound to contribute something towards success in the broader effort.

A number of people fail to realize that the motive of profit-earning in industry must always be subordinated to considerations of safety and stability; and the larger the undertaking the more likely is this principle to be observed. Not only is this true, but in all well-managed and substantial undertakings, especially those in key industries, a large proportion of the profits actually realized are devoted to the purpose of strengthening the position of the company, and with a view to providing steady rather than rapidly increasing dividends. It will be found on consideration that the dominant influence in shaping most of the outstanding developments in the industrial sphere and many of those in the political sphere is the search for that stability and security which is constantly disturbed by wide fluctuations in the price level.

In the political realm this effort assumes various shapes. In the early stages it takes the form of protection, bounties, and quotas. In its last stages it leads to direct State control and involves the complete supersession of the normal process of price-fixation by competitive influences. In Germany, Italy, Spain, Russia and Central Europe different systems are being tested out, each designed in some way to assume responsibility for the functions of industry and to control the natural tendency of prices to find their own level.

In the industrial sphere the most significant aspect of the quest for stability, and one especially outstanding since the War, has been the movement on the part of producers to group themselves in various forms of association such as trusts, combines, international cartels, etc., which differ only in the matter of the closeness and breadth of the contact.

The association may consist of some kind of working agreement between those engaged in producing and selling a similar article (horizontal combination) or manifest itself in a unified control over the various stages of production (vertical combination), commencing with, say, ownership of iron-ore and coal mines and limestone quarries, and thence supplying in the same unit blast-furnaces, rolling mills etc., the output from which will feed plant for the production of finished steel goods of every description. In its further development industrial combination embraces both forms, includes many associated and subsidiary businesses besides, and over-rides national boundaries. Sometimes association is carried to the stage in which a company having an independent legal existence is established in order to sell the entire output of a group of producers for their joint account.

It is true that at the present time combines and cartels are widely suspect: their star is clouded by recent happenings. This but serves to draw attention to the fact that the development of this form of organization is too immature to be free from many imperfections. This is not to say that their failings should be lightly dismissed; but before a sound conclusion on the subject can be reached it is necessary to consider the nature of the influences that have driven producers into association.

The first is excessive competition. The system of industry that proceeds by way of unregulated competition is always tending to resolve itself into a situation whereby a collection of producers, each as a rule with a capacity much in excess of his actual sales, compete one against the other in order to obtain a sufficient share of the market to pay costs and earn a profit. If one producer is particularly successful in securing a growing share of business, it is at the price of closing down a few rivals.

For this method, or lack of method, the combine substitutes the quota system, which allocates to each constituent concern its due proportion of the market. It is a mistake to suppose that competition and the incentive to improvement are thereby eliminated. Though each firm is limited to its quota, the savings which it is able to effect within its own organization are to its own advantage, while the fact that agreements are only concluded for a limited period means that each firm is constantly alive to the necessity for maintaining its position and keeping abreast of new development.

Apart from association of this kind the prosperity and very existence of every industrial undertaking is constantly threatened in ways other than the direct competition of producers engaged in the same business. There are the risks inherent in changes of taste, fashion, and custom, and those resulting from changes of process due to research work and invention; these may lead to ruinous losses to firms not able to make the necessary adjustments or not recognizing the necessity soon enough. Superimposed on these internal risks of industry is the constantly recurring menace of the trade cycle.

Against all these dangers the members of trade associations receive some measure of protection.

In regard to changes in taste and custom the resources and information at their disposal are such that no early disaster is threatened, and there is at least a good prospect of successful accommodation to the new conditions. Against sudden and overwhelming changes of process, the members of the combine are insured by reason of the fact that research work is generally undertaken as a joint enterprise. The pooling of research work, and—when it exists—of sales services and publicity expenses as well as the reduction in surplus plant and the standardization of the classes of goods produced, all tend to reduce the costs of production of the syndicated producers.

In these matters trades associations are endeavouring to combat the instability of particular prices, but of not less importance to them is their effort to alleviate some of the effects of recurring depressions. In this respect their forecasting is likely to be superior to that of the average small individual producer, while the ability to control and regulate output according to the needs of the time is infinitely superior to that of a large number of unco-ordinated independent units.

The combine is also able to adopt a more purposeful policy in regard to price reduction than would be possible with a small organization. By reducing prices in special lines according to the market situation, by fostering new sources of demand, and above all, by their greater financial resources, the inroads of the slump tend to be more firmly resisted by associations than by individual producers.[1] When full recognition has been

[1] Such is the conclusion formed by the group of experts who reported to the League of Nations Section on Economic Relations. *Vide* Report on the Economic Aspects of International Industrial Agreements.

accorded to the dangers and disintegrating tendencies of unregulated competition the critic of combination may well be asked, "What is the alternative?"

Is it conceivable that a host of small independent units engaged in anarchic competition can long survive against any form of planned and systematized production? If not it may be well to consider whether the advantages of combination outweigh the disadvantages, and whether the latter may not prove remediable. The special aspects to which experience of the past draws attention may be grouped under four headings: administration, finance, labour conditions and public interests.

The administrative element immediately focuses attention upon the heart of the matter. It is impossible to enter here upon a detailed discussion of the subject, but it will be readily recognized that the reaping of the advantages to be derived from large-scale organization in respect of division of labour, large-scale buying, marketing economies, technical improvement, planning of production and research organization to a large extent depend upon effective co-ordination. The magnitude of the problem will not be underestimated by those who are acquainted with the astonishing ramifications of some of the large international combines. Apart from successful co-ordination the large unit will become unwieldy, and the benefit of such economies as are achieved be outweighed by the superior mobility and dynamic of a smaller rival.[1] The whole problem of large-scale organization has, however, received a great deal of study and attention in recent years; even so it is probably only in its infancy. In this country, though considerable progress has been achieved latterly, it is generally accepted that our standards in this sphere are behind those of America and Germany. Perhaps the most common failing has been to imagine that a mere financial inter-locking in itself provides some natural assurance of an effectively co-ordinated organization. In actual fact this by no means follows. Many examples could be given where executive and competitive efficiency have been weakened by control passing into the hands of financiers without any special aptitude for industrial organization. Beyond this the problem of finding first-rate human talent will always remain. The difficulty is not alone the comparative rarity of first-rate ability, but of recognizing and making room for it when found. The revolutions that give Napoleons their chance are not to be encouraged on that account.

On the financial side the danger lies in the secrecy with which these huge combines operate. It is true that annual reports are published, but since the figures may

[1] "All sorts of problems of organization and co-ordination arise because the unit to be controlled is now large instead of small, is out of ear-shot, takes time, space, and forethought to manage. A mistake made by a platoon commander demands only an instantaneous 'As you were.' A mistake by an Army Commander may require days of labour to set right."—Extract from *The Structure of Competitive Industry*, by E. A. G. Robinson, M.A.

conceal more than they reveal, nobody is much the wiser. The shareholder is expected to live by faith rather than by sight, but has not infrequently found his faith misplaced. Though it may be seldom that the annual statement of accounts is actually misleading or worse, it is frequent that they are almost meaningless. It is beyond question that the confidence of the investor in large combines is seriously shaken. It is of great consequence to the community at large, as well as to the vital interest of the combines themselves, that this confidence should be fully restored.

The subject has recently received a good deal of attention from prominent members of the accountancy profession. There appears to be a wide measure of agreement that some amendment to the law as it now exists is demanded. Such differences of opinion as have arisen are largely concerned with how far improvement may be achieved apart from legal enactment.

The Society of Incorporated Accountants and Auditors recommends that a Holding Company having investments in subsidiary companies should be compelled to show in their accounts the ascertained profits and losses of all subsidiaries in so far as they have not been brought into the Profit and Loss Account of the Holding Company. Further, that in the Profit and Loss Accounts of all Companies debits and credits of an abnormal or extraneous character should be separately stated. Both suggestions appear to have definite value for promoting the end in view.

It will be accepted by everybody as a governing principle that combines of monopolist or quasi-monopolist character cannot be allowed to enrich themselves by price-raising tactics. So far there is ample evidence to prove that combination has tended on the whole to lower prices: in some of the instances where an attempt has been made to maintain an unduly high level the result has been a disastrous recoil on the heads of the guilty syndicates. It must not be forgotten that combines are always subject to potential competition induced by high prices and to the indirect competition of substitutional products, as well as to the direct competition of independent producers in greater or lesser numbers and importance. It is true that a different set of circumstances might lead to different results, but against this the weapon of publicity can always be held in reserve.

Lastly, labour has most to gain from improving the stability, prosperity and productive capacity of industry. As matters stand, a constant pressure is exerted on the wage level by the precariousness of profits, while inability to balance production and consumption is reflected in a high ratio of unemployment. Nor is a weakening of the human interest at all a necessary consequence of large-scale undertakings. On the contrary organized welfare work, hygiene and the provision of recreational facilities is more generally practised by the larger and wealthier combines than by scattered and weaker producers. Some of the large concerns have also been able to demonstrate that a high degree of *esprit de corps* may be inculcated by fostering the human relationships, though this aspect has not as a rule received the attention it deserves. Most of the scientific study of working conditions also comes from the side of large-scale production: such things as industrial psychology with its motion study, rest-pauses, and arrangement of work, all have their value in improving the health and contentment of the personnel, while the specialized training and education which is sometimes provided tends to improve the average efficiency. On the whole, therefore, so far from being inimical to labour interests, large-scale organization should tend in the direction of substantially raising the wage level, while offering greater security and better conditions of employment. Against this it must be admitted that the immediate effect of combination and association is to lead to dismissals, and this short-term effect in reducing employment needs special consideration at a time like the present, and would in some cases call for the postponement of otherwise desirable economies.

No attempt has been made here to enumerate or distinguish between the different forms of trade combination in any detail. It must, of course, be recognized that large-scale production or organization is not equally applicable throughout the whole sphere of industrial production, but its variety of application is such that its scope is sufficiently broad to justify the employment of the term as a generalized conception.

It should be added that the complete elimination of the small producer in syndicated industries is neither necessary nor desirable. His success will not be likely to endanger the stability of the whole structure and, frequently, will be met by absorption on favourable terms in the wider organization.

CONCLUSIONS

Our examination of the economic situation discloses the primary aim of the whole industrial and political effort as being the attempt to secure a greater measure of general stability as a basis on which to develop the pent-up possibilities of modern society. The means of achieving the desired result are being sought in two distinct spheres, by independent but complementary effort. The economist and the banker must seek to provide a more stable standard of value which statesmanship will endeavour to secure against external disturbance. It is for the industrialist on his part to devise improved means of conducting and developing large-scale organization. There are good grounds for believing that in recent years monetary art has progressed to a point where the extent and violence of industrial fluctuation can be diminished. Beyond this the theoretical difficulty of achieving a stable standard of value is very great, but even if overcome, the path leading to success in the practical world must inevitably be chequered.

The independent effort of the industrialist to regulate production according to the conditions of demand will, therefore, proceed from a desire to mitigate the effects of the trade cycle as well as from that relating to the circumstances of a particular line of business.

It is abundantly clear that the days of unbridled competition are over. Its drawbacks are too strong to be ignored: the wastage of productive capacity, the constant menace to the survival of individual firms, and the steady downward pressure exerted on profits and wages. From these repressive influences industry and society, as a whole, must inevitably obtain relief or succumb to the practical achievements of a State-systematized production.

We are faced therefore with a choice between improved organization, monetary and industrial, and a rigid State control. The latter would supersede competition and the determining function of prices by assuming responsibility for and regulating the industrial effort of all undertakings and individuals.

A system of this kind has considerable economic defects (apart from disadvantages which most people will consider more vital, namely, that rigid control must inevitably make severe inroads upon the individual's right of free expression in word and act). A large body of autonomous producers is far more likely to initiate and be receptive of new ideas and methods and to consider and minister to changes in the public taste than a supreme central executive. If the world is too big and too interlinked for a policy of selfish individualism narrowly conceived, it is also too complex and too changing for its functions to be adequately controlled or stimulated from a central headquarters.

Large industrial groups will, however, pave the way to a more conscious direction of industrial effort. Widespread connections, superior forecasting, and ability to regulate production in an orderly manner all assist the attainment of this object.

In this discussion political considerations have been deliberately reduced to a minimum. Progress in regard to fundamental principles is more likely to be achieved by so doing. The precise form of relationship which should subsist between the large industrial units and the State will be variously defined by persons of differing political complexion.

There is little doubt that this broad line of development affords considerable latitude to political ideas. Future years will almost certainly demonstrate the fact by reason of divergences in actual policy in the different nations of the world.

In this country our specific and typical contribution to the problem of public administration has been the formation of various public bodies charged with responsibilities in the public interest. Immediate instances are at hand in the Bank of England, the British Broadcasting Corporation, Port of London Authority and Electricity Commission. But in actual fact a number of other functions are similarly administered in the spheres of education, hospitals and public utilities. There is thus nothing contrary to the character or tendencies of British economic and political development in the rise of large-scale industrial units.

The final conclusion may legitimately be drawn that a great increase in the material welfare of all classes of society is a practical possibility of the present era, but is dependent upon success in the sphere of monetary reform and further progress in the orderly development of large-scale industrial organization.

STATISTICAL APPENDIX

PRICE INDICES *

Wholesale Prices and Cost of Living

Date	United Kingdom		United States of America		France		Germany†	
	Wholesale	Cost of Living July	Wholesale	Cost of Living	Wholesale	Cost of Living Paris	Wholesale	Cost of Living
	1913=100 Economist	1914=100	1913=100 Bureau of Labour	1923=100	1913=100 Official	1914=100	1913=100	1914=100
1929	127·6	164	136·5	100·0	124·1	113	137·2	153·8
1930	108·2	158	123·8	96·2	108·7	118	124·6	147·3
1931 March	91·1	147	108·9	89·1	97·8	120	113·9	137·7
September	89·6	145	102·0	85·6	86·9	115	108·6	134·0
1932 January	90·0	147	96·4	81·4	82·3	108‡	100·0	124·5
February	92·2	146	95·0	80·1	83·7	—	99·8	122·3
March	89·9	144	94·6	79·6	84·9	108	99·8	122·4
April	86·3	143	93·8	78·8	84·3	—	98·4	121·7
May	83·3	143	—	—	83·7	—	97·2	121·1

* League of Nations Monthly Bulletin of Statistics.
† In terms of present currency.
‡ December 1931 quarter.

APPENDIX

THE COURSE OF AMERICAN COMMON STOCK PRICES

Stock	1926 Highest	1926 Lowest	1927 Highest	1927 Lowest	1928 Highest	1928 Lowest	1929 Highest	1929 Lowest	1930 Highest	1930 Lowest	1931 Highest	1931 Lowest
American Tel. and Tel.	151	139$\frac{5}{8}$	185$\frac{1}{2}$	149$\frac{1}{4}$	211	172	310$\frac{1}{4}$	193$\frac{1}{4}$	274$\frac{1}{4}$ April	170$\frac{3}{8}$ Dec.	201$\frac{3}{4}$ Feb.	121$\frac{1}{8}$ Dec.
Drug Incorporated	—	—	—	—	120$\frac{1}{8}$	80	126$\frac{1}{8}$	69	87$\frac{7}{8}$ March	57$\frac{5}{8}$ Dec.	78$\frac{3}{4}$ March	42$\frac{5}{8}$ Oct.
Eastman Kodak	136$\frac{3}{4}$	106$\frac{5}{8}$	175$\frac{1}{4}$	126$\frac{1}{4}$	194$\frac{1}{4}$	163	264$\frac{3}{4}$	150	255$\frac{1}{4}$ April	142$\frac{1}{8}$ Dec.	185$\frac{3}{4}$ Feb.	77 Dec.
General Electric	95$\frac{1}{2}$	79	146$\frac{5}{8}$	81	221$\frac{1}{2}$	124	63$\frac{1}{4}$ (split 4 for 1)	55$\frac{1}{4}$	95$\frac{3}{8}$ April	41$\frac{1}{2}$ Dec.	54$\frac{1}{4}$ Feb.	22$\frac{7}{8}$ Dec.
General Motors	173$\frac{1}{2}$	137$\frac{1}{4}$	282$\frac{1}{4}$	145$\frac{1}{2}$	224$\frac{3}{4}$	130	91$\frac{1}{4}$ ($10 par stock)	33$\frac{1}{2}$	54$\frac{1}{4}$ April	31$\frac{1}{2}$ Nov.	48 March	21$\frac{3}{8}$ Dec.
Kennecott Copper	64$\frac{1}{4}$	49$\frac{3}{4}$	90$\frac{3}{4}$	60	156	80$\frac{1}{8}$	104$\frac{7}{8}$	49$\frac{7}{8}$	62$\frac{3}{4}$ Feb.	20$\frac{5}{8}$ Dec.	31$\frac{1}{8}$ Feb.	9$\frac{5}{8}$ Dec.
Montgomery Ward	82	56	123$\frac{1}{4}$	60$\frac{7}{8}$	439$\frac{7}{8}$	117	156$\frac{7}{8}$ (new stock issue)	42$\frac{7}{8}$	49$\frac{7}{8}$ Jan.	15$\frac{7}{8}$ Dec.	29$\frac{1}{4}$ Feb.	6$\frac{7}{8}$ Dec.
Radio Corp.	61$\frac{3}{8}$	32	101	41$\frac{1}{8}$	420	85$\frac{1}{4}$	549 (old stock split 5 for 1)	26	69$\frac{3}{8}$ April	11$\frac{3}{8}$ Dec.	27$\frac{1}{2}$ Feb.	5$\frac{7}{8}$ Dec.
United States Steel	160$\frac{1}{2}$	113$\frac{5}{8}$	160$\frac{1}{4}$	111$\frac{3}{8}$	172$\frac{3}{4}$	132$\frac{7}{8}$	261$\frac{3}{4}$	150	198$\frac{3}{4}$ April	134$\frac{3}{4}$ Dec.	152$\frac{3}{8}$ Feb.	36 Dec.
Westinghouse Elect.	79$\frac{1}{2}$	65	94$\frac{3}{4}$	67$\frac{7}{8}$	144	88$\frac{1}{8}$	292$\frac{5}{8}$	100	201$\frac{1}{8}$ April	88$\frac{1}{8}$ Dec.	107$\frac{3}{4}$ Feb.	22$\frac{1}{4}$ Dec.
Woolworth	128	120$\frac{1}{4}$	198$\frac{1}{2}$	117$\frac{3}{4}$	225$\frac{3}{4}$	175$\frac{1}{2}$	234 (old stock split 2$\frac{1}{2}$ for 1)	52$\frac{1}{4}$	72$\frac{5}{8}$ Jan. 2	51$\frac{1}{2}$ Jan. 17	72$\frac{1}{4}$ Aug.	35 Dec.

AMERICAN WHOLESALE PRICES*

	Unit	April 1913	April 1920	April 1929	April 1930	April 1931	April 1932
COPPER—							
Electrolytic, Early Delivery, New York	Cents per lb.	15.50	18.75	17.87½	13.87½	9.87½	5.62¼
CORN—							
No. 2 Mixed, Chicago	Dollars per bushel	0.55½	1.68	0.93¾	0.81	0.60½	0.33½
COTTON—							
Middling, Spot, New Orleans	Cents per lb.	12.50	41.50	19.52	15.40	9.90	6.26
HIDES—							
Green Salted Packers, No. 1, Heavy Native Steers, Chicago	Cents per lb.	17	35	15	14	9	4⅞
IRON AND STEEL—							
Pig-iron, Basic, Valley Furnace	Dollars per gross ton	15.75	42.00	18.00	18.50	16.50	14.50
STEEL BILLETS—							
Open Hearth, Pittsburgh	Dollars per gross ton	29.00	65.00	34.00	33.00	30.00	27.00

PETROLEUM—							
Crude at well, Penns.	Dollars per barrel	2·50	6·10	4·00	2·80	1·85	1·82
RUBBER—							
Plantation Ribbed smoked Sheets, New York	Dollars per lb.	0·97	0·46	0·21¾	0·14¾	0·06⅝	0·03
SILK—							
White 13–15D Japan Crack XX, New York	Dollars per lb.	3·49	9·51	5·05	4·45	2·55	1·40
TIN—							
Straits, New York	Cents per lb.	48·00	62·50	45·20	36·30	25·25	18·60
WHEAT—							
No. 1, Northern Spring, Minneapolis	Dollars per bushel	0·86⅜	3·01	1·20⅞	1·03¾	0·80¼	0·71⅛
No. 2, Red Winter, Chicago	Dollars per bushel	1·04	2·75	1·31	1·08¾	0·84⅛	0·60⅛
WOOL—							
Ohio ¼ blood	Dollars per lb.	0·46	1·10	0·84	0·55	0·40	0·31

* Figures compiled by Guaranty Trust Company of New York.

SALIENT FIGURES FROM CENTRAL BANKS RETURNS

(Extracted from the *Economist* summaries of various dates)

(000's *omitted*)

UNITED STATES FEDERAL RESERVE BANKS

	April 25, 1929	April 24, 1930	April 30, 1931	April 28, 1932
Resources				
Total Gold Reserves	2,798,580	3,048,530	3,174,710	3,014,530
Total Bills Discounted	974,510	211,490	155,150	531,820
Total United States Government Securities	149,780	527,390	598,310	1,191,230
Total Bills and Securities	1,280,600	1,004,960	923,570	1,773,740
Liabilities				
Federal Reserve Notes in Actual Circulation	1,652,560	1,518,340	1,527,740	2,526,570
Deposits—Member Bank—Reserve Accounts	2,290,220	2,363,310	2,407,530	2,114,420
Total Deposits	2,350,080	2,422,190	2,462,840	2,234,200
Ratio of Total Reserves to Deposit and Federal Reserve Note Liabilities combined	74·3 %	81·8 %	84·0 %	67·9 %

APPENDIX

THE REICHSBANK

	April 27, 1929	April 30, 1930	April 23, 1931	April 23, 1932
Assets				
Gold	1,891,575	2,565,502	2,347,505	859,925
Reserve in Foreign Currencies	99,372	327,384	132,083	129,045
Bills of Exchange and Cheques	2,926,597	2,016,121	1,456,250	2,896,318
Liabilities				
Notes in Circulation	4,631,496	4,664,194	3,684,824	3,875,165
Other Liabilities (not Capital and Reserve)	875,773	698,554	714,925	1,064,933
Cover of Note Circulation	43·0 %	62·0 %	70·6 %	25·5 %

BANK OF FRANCE

	April 26, 1929	April 24, 1930	April 24, 1931	April 22, 1932
Assets				
Gold	35,788,083	42,350,815	55,615,943	77,480,944
Foreign Assets	27,025,399	25,655,181	26,305,362	12,359,371
Liabilities				
Notes in Circulation	62,847,740	70,770,213	77,230,864	81,145,445
Public Deposits	11,875,758	6,553,930	11,679,547	3,235,149
Private Deposits	6,858,828	7,666,101	11,724,890	25,636,328

BALANCE OF TRADE *

It is important to emphasize that the figures below refer only to transactions on income account *and not to* capital movements.

(In million £s)

	1929	1930	1931
Excess of imports of merchandise and silver bullion and specie	381	386	411
Estimated excess of Government receipts from overseas†	24	19	16
Estimated net National shipping income‡	130	105	80§
Estimated net income from overseas investments	250	220	165
Estimated net receipts from short interest and commissions	65	55	30
Estimated net receipts from other sources	15	15	10
Total	484	414	301
Estimated total credit or debit balance on items specified above	+ 103	+ 28	− 110
Excess of exports (+) or imports (−) of gold bullion and specie	+ 15	− 5	+ 35

* Board of Trade Estimates as published in the *Board of Trade Journal*.
† Including some items on loan accounts.
‡ Including disbursements by foreign ships in British ports.
§ Average tonnage of vessels laid up about one million tons more than in 1930.

INDEX

Acceptances, 27, 71, 72, 118
AMERICA—
  Bank Credit Act, 114
  Brokers' Loans, 45, 47, 51, 55
  Budget, 81
  Car production, 48
  Foreign Loans, 30, 45, 74, 75, 96
  Gold movements, 30, 68, 82, 106
  Hoover Moratorium, 38, 74
Australia, 23, 24, 102
Austria, 39, 60, 110, 125

Bank of International Settlements, 36, 39, 74, 143, 157
Bulgaria, 110, 125

Cartels, 163
Carter-Glass, 115
Coffee, 17
Combination, 163
Compensated dollar, 160
Copper, 19
Credit Anstalt, 39, 73
Credit cycle, 153
Czecho-Slovakia, 62, 122

Danubian countries, 123
Dawes Plan, 34, 60, 121

Exchange Equalisation Fund, 87, 88, 93

FRANCE
  Agricultural policy, 22, 109
  Bank of France, 39, 41, 74, 75, 108
  Bourse values, 34, 54, 108
  Budget, 80

FRANCE—*continued*
  Currency, 11, 60, 62
  Foreign Loans, 30, 85, 96, 110
  Gold movements, 28, 68, 82, 106
"Frozen Credit," 75, 85, 112

GERMANY—
  Darmstadter Bank, 74, 118
  Price fixation, 120
  Reichsbank, 74, 75, 118
  Unemployment, 121
GREAT BRITAIN—
  Balance of payments, 83, 84, 92
  Budget, 70, 76, 86, 87
  Death duties, 71
  Gold movements, 25, 26, 50, 75, 77
  Sterling exchange, 26, 60, 73, 78, 85, 90, 97, 105

Hungary, 41, 60, 62, 124

India, 12, 24, 102
Italy, 62, 127, 163

Keynes, J. M., 33, 131
Kreuger, I., 55

League of Nations, 41, 54, 60, 125, 126, 166

Macmillan Committee, 57, 69, 70, 149, 150, 158
May, Sir George, 70, 76

Nitrate, 19

"Offsetting," 32

Open-Market operations, 31, 98, 159
Oustric Group, 108

Paper pulp, 19
Power-farming, 19
Purchasing-Power Parity, 91, 101

Research, Industrial, 165, 166
Restriction, 59, 129, 165
Robinson, E. A. G., 168
Roumania, 110, 124
Rubber, 16, 58
Russia, 21, 163

Savings, 132, 140, 159
Short-term deposits, 69, 72
Silver, 12, 13
Sterilization, 31, 68
Sugar, 18

Treaty of Versailles, 34, **123**

War Loan, 5 per cent, 139
Wheat—
    Prices, 22, 124
    Production, 19, 22

Young Plan, 35, 121

For Product Safety Concerns and Information please contact our EU representative GPSR@taylorandfrancis.com
Taylor & Francis Verlag GmbH, Kaufingerstraße 24, 80331 München, Germany

www.ingramcontent.com/pod-product-compliance
Lightning Source LLC
Chambersburg PA
CBHW050637300426
44112CB00012B/1834